Sex, Drugs, Gambling, & Chocolate

SEX, DRUGS, GAMBLING, & CHOCOLATE

A Workbook for Overcoming Addictions

_____

A. Thomas Horvath, Ph.D.

_____

Impact Publishers, Inc.
SAN LUIS OBISPO, CALIFORNIA

Publisher's Note
This publication is designed to provide accurate and authoritative information in regard to the subject matter covered. It is sold with the understanding that the publisher is not engaged in rendering psychological, medical, or other professional services. If expert assistance or counseling is needed, the services of a competent professional should be sought.

Library of Congress Cataloging in Publication Data

Horvath, A. Thomas.
        Sex, drugs, gambling, & chocolate : a workbook for overcoming addictions / A. Thomas Horvath.
        p. cm.
    Includes bibliographical references and index.
    ISBN 1-886230-15-3 (alk. paper)
    1. Compulsive behavior -- Treatment -- Handbooks, manuals, etc. 2. Substance abuse -- Treatment -- Handbooks, manuals, etc. 3. Self-care, Health -- Handbooks, manuals, etc. I. Title. II. Title: Sex, drugs, gambling, and chocolate
    RC533 .H66 1998
    616.86'06 -- ddc21   98 - 44117
                                                                 CIP

Printed in the United States of America on acid-free paper
Cover design by Catharine Kornreich, San Luis Obispo, California
Impact Publishers and colophon are registered trademarks of Impact Publishers, Inc.

Published by ***Impact ⬥ Publishers, Inc.***
POST OFFICE BOX 910
SAN LUIS OBISPO, CALIFORNIA 93406-0910

Sex, Drugs, Gambling, & Chocolate
A. Thomas Horvath, Ph.D.

Contents

Foreword: G. Alan Marlatt, Ph.D.
Foreword: Reid K. Hester, Ph.D.
Acknowledgements

Foreword

There is growing recognition in the United States of what other countries have known for many years: There are many levels and subtypes of addictive behavior and many ways to change them. The terms "addict" and "alcoholic" may be useful in some cases, but there is a wide range of addictive problems for which these terms are inappropriate or even harmful. Although 12-step groups such as Alcoholics Anonymous are often helpful, many individuals with addictive problems are inappropriate for such groups or have legitimate reasons for not attending them.

It is not possible for one workbook to contain the solution to addictive problems for all individuals, and this workbook does not claim to contain such a solution. What it does offer could be invaluable, however, to the individual who is searching for a reasoned and scientifically researched set of methods for overcoming addiction. For that individual this workbook might even be lifesaving. It remains difficult in the United States even to be informed that the ideas in this workbook exist. In other words, you are lucky to have found it!

A major feature of this workbook is its acceptance of the philosophy of harm reduction. Harm reduction focuses on helping the individual move toward problem resolution, even if that resolution does not occur entirely or all at once. Moderation or abstinence is a personal decision, and abstinence is not a rigid requirement. The approach incorporates the ideas that "something is better than nothing," and that a small step is often easier to take than, and sets the stage for, a large one. Harm reduction is a practical approach that acknowledges the differences between individuals and respects their capacity to shape their own lives.

Fortunately, information about alternative approaches to addictive problems is becoming more widespread. This workbook is an important step in informing the public of its options. I expect that there will always be a place for the most common approach to treatment in the U.S. today: acceptance of addiction as a disease, acceptance of powerlessness, attendance at 12-step meetings, and so forth. But, as this workbook and the ideas it presents become more well known, individuals who recognize their own addictive behaviors will also know that there are various methods for changing them, not just the traditional ones. If you are ready for an alternative approach to overcoming addiction, this workbook could make a big difference in your life!

G. Alan Marlatt, Ph.D.

Professor of Psychology, University of Washington
Director of Addictive Behaviors Research Center

Foreword

My colleagues and I have been reviewing, summarizing, and writing about addiction treatment research for two decades now. What we have observed is both encouraging and disturbing. The research clearly shows that there is no single approach which is superior to all others. Rather, there are a number of alternatives that are consistently supported by scientific research. These treatments have been developed and tested primarily in the last two decades and are the best that science has to offer for those seeking to overcome alcohol problems. That's the good news. The not so good news is that alcohol treatment programs in the U.S. have only slowly begun to offer these treatments. Also, the average person, not inclined to spend hours in medical libraries, would have difficulty learning about these approaches or even learning that they exist. In a country that prides itself on technological and scientific sophistication, the best that science has to offer for overcoming addiction is not widely known.

If you are considering treatment for yourself or another, you need to be aware of these alternatives. Fortunately, some psychologists and other addiction professionals offer scientifically based alternatives. I hope that in time these alternatives will become more well known. This workbook is a good place to learn about them.

This workbook offers an in-depth guide to a number of scientifically supported approaches for overcoming addiction. But don't just take my word for it. Try these strategies yourself and see how they can be helpful to you. You, too, can overcome your addictions and enhance your life.

Reid K. Hester, Ph.D.

Director, Research Division
Behavior Therapy Associates
www.lobo.net/~rhester

Research Associate Professor
Department of Psychology, University of New Mexico
Albuquerque, New Mexico

Senior Editor, *Handbook of Alcoholism Treatment Approaches: Effective Alternatives*, 2nd edition. Allyn & Bacon, (1995)

Acknowledgements

I hope that it will be reassuring to the reader that none of the major ideas in this workbook are new, or original to the author. The purpose of this workbook is to draw together ideas and techniques that have been well studied and used in the field of addiction psychology and to present them in one readable workbook.

Sometimes, of course, it is exciting to have the very newest product (or idea). However, we feel more secure with established products if they are known to work well. Fortunately, the typical reader of this workbook may get to experience both excitement and security. There could be the excitement of newness (because the ideas herein are not well known), yet the secure feeling of using what is well tested.

The ideas in this workbook are drawn from a vast primary and secondary scientific literature. Only a few gateways to that literature are listed in the Bibliography and Resources appendix. As noted in Chapter 6, learning is primarily a social experience. Many individuals have contributed to my education about the ideas in this workbook and to the matrix of support that has been the foundation of my education and other accomplishments. There is space here only to acknowledge the most noteworthy of them. I am deeply grateful for their help, without which this workbook and many other aspects of my life would not have been possible. I am, however, solely responsible for any errors herein. This workbook is not an official statement of any of the organizations with which I am affiliated.

This workbook originated in 1989 as a self-help article entitled "Coping with Addiction." Colleagues who contributed to my thinking at that time include Alan Marlatt, Chris Padesky, Aaron Beck, Karen Sorensen, Kathleen Mooney and Craig Wiese. In 1985 I obtained training from the New Horizons addiction treatment program and for several years had extensive contact with colleagues in that organization.

The second version of this workbook appeared in 1994 as the "Addictive Behavior Workbook," written while I was a consultant to Mercy Hospital, San Diego, and Palomar Hospital, Escondido. The Mercy staff was directed by Rod Munoz, Karenlee Robinson and Jerry Gold. The Palomar staff was directed by Jim Greeley and Susan Linback. Both staffs provided a professional and congenial working environment.

The third version appeared in 1996 as the "Addictive Behavior Change (ABC) Workbook" and was written for the drop-in support group (the ABC Workshop) I have been conducting since 1995. I am deeply grateful to participants in the ABC Workshop and my clients, who have provided numerous insights about the ideas in this workbook and how to present them.

Three organizations have been central to my professional education. SMART Recovery has allowed me to have contact with hundreds of individuals desiring to accomplish a self-reliant recovery from addiction and dozens of like-minded professionals, especially Hank Robb, Michler Bishop, Phil Tate, Vince Fox, Joe Gerstein, Robert Taylor, Jeff Schaler, Bill Ravin, Steve McCullough, Nick Rajacic, John Boren, and Judith Lloyd. Shari Allwood, the SMART Manager of Member and Network Services, is an organizational and interpersonal genius. I get to observe firsthand the inspiring persistence of San Diego SMART Recovery Coordinators and members.

The American Psychological Association's Division on Addictions (Division 50) has afforded the opportunity to learn from dozens of colleagues, especially Mark Goldman, Bob Zucker, Bruce Liese, Jim Sorensen, and Sandy Brown.

As part of an organization sponsored consultation series, and at other times, I have had the opportunity to consult with many senior members of the Association for Advancement of Behavior Therapy, including Reid Hester, David Abrams, Barbara McCrady, Mark Sobell, Linda Sobell, Jalie Tucker, Tim O'Farrell, and Lorraine Collins.

My colleagues at Practical Recovery Services (PRS) are Karen Sorensen, Bob Hoyk, Jeff Jones, and Kris Figueroa. They have helped me take the ideas of this workbook and shape them into a multi-service treatment center. I am extremely fortunate to be able to work with such gifted, dedicated and creative individuals. Karen Sorensen has been a friend, supporter, colleague and trusted advisor for over a decade. She exemplifies for me the meaning of the term "professional."

Detailed comments on early drafts were provided by Karen Sorensen, Bob Hoyk, Kris Figueroa, Craig Wiese, Lloyd Hill, John Boren, and Edward Zuckerman. Detailed information on specific issues was provided by Derek Cross and Doug Braun Harvey.

ACKNOWLEDGEMENTS

As to broad influences not necessarily connected directly with this workbook but crucial to its existence, I am grateful for the continued love and attention from my mother and father, sisters, and extended family. My parents helped instill and support a love of learning. Jack Wendle, my high school history teacher and tennis coach, introduced me to many new ideas. St. John's College and its Great Books curriculum expanded my intellectual horizon considerably. Members of my dissertation committee at the California School of Professional Psychology, Dick Gevirtz, Dick Kelly, and David Hord, were consistently helpful and inspiring. Discussions and friendship with Russ Federman and Steve Seagren are an ongoing pleasure of life. My office partners and associates over the years have been essential to creating a happy and supportive working environment and have included John Grabel, Nancy Haller, Bonny Hammell, Craig Wiese, Brenda Johnson, Sherry Cook, Bob Westermeyer, Barbara Alvarez Warren, and Michael Coe. The following individuals have been helpful at various times and in a variety of ways: Paul Cleary, Jan and Rick Farley, Dick Greene, Maria Andujo Hanger, Susan Jasin, Ellen Landfear, Ann and Gary Lawson, Carol LeBeau, Tom Marra, Penny Masters, Bill Mead, Art Pammenter, Barbara Severance, Mary Stamler, Jim Street, Alison Urbank, Dan Valentine, and Mary Vattimo.

My editor, Bob Alberti, and the staff at Impact Publishers have completed their work quietly but effectively. It has been a pleasure to work with them.

My wife and children have tolerated the temporary obsession that writing induces in me. Time with them is an example of the "higher satisfactions" I refer to in Chapter 11.

Tom Horvath
La Jolla, CA
August, 1998

Sex, Drugs, Gambling, Chocolate, ...

...alcohol
wine
cigarettes
cigars
religion
overeating
slot machines
television
videos
food
fortified wine
the lottery
ice cream
dessert
candy
video games
liquor
poker
card games
the internet
chat rooms
net surfing
relationships
work
cocaine
roulette
heroin
morphine
LSD
pot
crack
pills
barbiturates
benzodiazepines
amphetamine
networking
crystal

talking
dating
snacking
beer
junk food
reading
going out
political activity
talking about myself
shopping
spending
meeting new people
cars
pulling my hair
pleasing others
exercise
running
steroids
soap operas
sitcoms
whining
976 & 900 numbers
shoplifting
chewing tobacco
setting fires
anger
colas
coffee
diet pills
pets
collecting things
saving things
caring for others
newspaper reading
picking at myself
comfort
taking it easy

clothes
ecstasy
MDMA
romance novels
pornography
going to bars
sports bars
watching sports
strip joints
prostitutes
looking good
music
daydreams
fantasy
codeine
methadone
PCP
crank
driving fast
orderliness
cleanliness
sports betting
lotto
purging
laxatives
grooming
affairs
romance
craps
preparation
novelty
anonymous sex
masturbation
fire-setting
prostitution
dancing
making money

Introduction

Every man has business and desire, such as it is.
        -- William Shakespeare (1564-1616)
        Hamlet, Act I, Scene v

Every man put himself into triumph;
some to dance, some to make bonfires,
each man to what sport and revels his addiction leads him.
        -- William Shakespeare (1564-1616)
        Othello, Act II, Scene ii

Did you read the list on the opposite page? Isn't the variety of addictive substances and activities amazing? Once you have read a few chapters of this workbook, I hope you will agree that nearly everyone has an "addiction" of some type. If you have one, large or small, and want to do something about it, keep reading! This workbook presents a "common sense" approach to overcoming addiction, one that is also supported by scientific research.

      We begin with two fundamental ideas: (1) addiction, in its varying degrees, is an extreme version of habit; and (2) overcoming addiction occurs using the same processes we use to change other habits. To be sure, severe addiction can result in horrendous consequences, but even severe addiction can be changed using normal human change processes.

Although some individuals become more addicted than others, everyone slips from habit into addiction (broadly defined) at times. Both are normal, part of being human.

The ordinary processes that change either habits or addictions include, among others:
⇒ increasing self-awareness
⇒ identifying and resolving conflict
⇒ discovering and developing alternative behaviors
⇒ experiencing support from others
⇒ not acting on temptation
⇒ being persistent

Habit change is a psychological problem, and addiction also can be viewed as a psychological problem requiring a psychological solution.

In the *traditional approach* to addiction, used by almost all addiction treatment and support groups in the United States, addiction is viewed as a medical and spiritual problem -- a disease -- and attending Alcoholics Anonymous (AA) or other "12-step" groups is necessary for recovery. AA's 12 steps describe how recovery occurs by turning over one's will and one's life to the care of a "higher power" (or God, as understood by each individual).

This workbook was written to provide an *alternative approach* for those who might prefer one. In the remainder of this Introduction I present an overview and brief justification of this alternative.

What Is Addiction?

'To addict' is derived from a Latin root meaning to assign to, or to surrender. There is no definitive contemporary definition of addiction. We will use a "working definition" which is consistent with what is known about addiction treatment and with common sense.

Addiction is repeated involvement with anything, despite excessive costs, because of craving.

The three central concepts here are "anything," "excessive," and "craving." Let's work backwards.

Craving. Craving can be a complete experience: feelings, thoughts, sensations, images. When craving occurs, you strongly desire a specific substance or activity. You have an urge for it, get jumpy and twitchy, feel you can't go on without it, start losing interest in everything else, recall a previous "high" and look forward to the next one. Craving is a kind of tunnel vision. As it gets stronger, you perceive less and less of everything else and become increasingly focused on getting back to your addiction. If nothing significant stops you, that's what you do. Chapters 8 through 10 will focus on how to cope with craving.

Excessive. All involvements have a cost. If the cost is in proportion to the benefits received, we are satisfied. If the cost is relatively low, it's a bargain. In addiction, the cost is relatively high. Although there are still benefits in addiction (we'll elaborate on this in Chapters 3 and 4), addiction is the opposite of a bargain. In *addiction,* repeated involvement occurs because the tunnel vision of craving momentarily hinders us from recognizing the discrepancy between cost and benefits. In *mild addiction,* cost clearly but slightly exceeds the benefits. In *severe addiction,* the difference between costs and benefits is dramatic. A habit is repeated involvement when costs and benefits are about equal.

Anything. Although addiction has usually meant substance addiction, in recent years there is recognition of addictions involving gambling, sex, spending, relationships, and other activities. It now appears that any substance or activity (i.e., *anything*) could lead to addiction, because addiction is a type of *relationship* between an individual and the substance or activity. If you need suggestions about substances or activities to consider, look at the list of addictions opposite page 1. This does not present a definitive list (that would be impossible), but many common addictions are listed. *The individual is an active contributor to the addictive relationship*, and not a passive victim of a substance or activity. If we were at the mercy of certain substances or activities, everyone sufficiently exposed to them would become addicted, but this does not happen.

Consider phobias. Most of us are exposed to elevators, freeway driving, heights, insects, and other aspects of daily life. Only a few of us develop phobias (excessive fears) to these objects. Although it is possible to develop a phobia to anything, in practice most phobias occur to predictable objects and situations. These phobias are predictable because their objects or situations are fearsome in at least some degree to most people, because of the possible (even if unlikely) connection to survival. If elevator cables break, an auto accident occurs, a fall occurs, or you get bitten by a disease carrying insect, death may result. We get phobic about these kinds of objects. We typically don't get phobic about desks, books, sidewalks, or other almost-always-benign objects.

Similarly, addictions tend to develop to substances or activities that strongly influence emotions. Substances that influence emotion via physiological (physical) actions are called *psychoactive.* But even substances which are not "physiologically psychoactive" can become "psychologically psychoactive" because of learned associations to them. The same process could occur for activities. I have observed (a few) addictions to non-psychoactive substances, the negative consequences of which were substantial.

If addiction is a relationship, then there is no one "most addictive" substance or activity. Heroin or crack cocaine are often suggested to be the most addictive substances. Although more individuals might seek a second experience with these substances than might with some other substances (although no one has ever proven this), it also is beyond doubt that many individuals do not seek a first experience, and many other individuals, after one or several experiences with heroin or crack cocaine, do not seek more. Furthermore, those who have quit heroin and cigarettes, or crack cocaine and cigarettes, state that even though they enjoyed heroin or cocaine more, the cigarettes were harder to stop. Like all relationships, addictive relationships have many components.

For a particular individual there may be a "most addictive" relationship. This is often called the "drug of choice." Why this drug (or activity) is most favored is undoubtedly a complicated interweaving of biology, personal history, personality and circumstance that is well beyond our current ability to explain. We are also not able to explain how individuals with a drug of choice and possibly several additional addictions may also have a mild or non-existent positive response to other "addictive" substances or activities. Although we might be addicted to almost anything, we are usually very far from being addicted to everything.

In summary, an addiction can develop to any substance or activity, but addictions tend to develop only to those which under normal circumstances influence emotion. Even though an individual may have several addictions, he or she does not have all addictions.

There are many behaviors that at first glance appear to fit this working definition of addiction. A college freshman who ends up in the emergency room after his first alcohol binge may not have been repeatedly involved with alcohol (although he may soon be). A medical patient on opiates for pain control probably does not crave the next injection for the "high," but simply wants a reduction in pain. An occasional low stakes poker player may incur a minor expense when she loses, but the pleasure of gambling in this manner, for this individual, outweighs the cost, so it is not excessive. This last example illustrates how addiction is highly dependent on the context in which it occurs. What is a minor expense for one individual might not be for another.

The working definition of addiction is similar in some respects to the traditional definition of addiction (or alcoholism) as a disease. The "three C's" of the traditional definition are craving, consequences and (loss of) control. However, the traditional definition is all-or-none (you either are an addict/alcoholic or not), craving is often suggested to be uncontrollable, and moderate involvement with the addiction is considered impossible.

The facts contradict this disease model of addiction. There is a range (actually multiple ranges) of addictive behavior. There is no clear dividing line where addiction begins. Craving is fully controllable (otherwise addiction is a hopeless situation--but it's not!). Moderate involvement is possible and worth considering.

The working definition of addiction also suggests the possibility of a positive addiction (or good habit). Positive addiction is regular involvement with a substance or activity, accompanied by a minor degree of craving, with the benefits of involvement outweighing the costs. Habit is repeated involvement when costs and benefits are about equal. Ironically, the resolution of (harmful) addiction involves the development of positive addictions.

Consider toothbrushing. If you brush regularly (and I hope you do!), but miss a brushing, do you begin to crave the opportunity to brush? I do, and I believe many others do. The craving is not strong, but there is a sense of having missed something. As severe addictions develop, positive addictions drop out of the individual's life (including tooth brushing!), and the restoration of these behaviors (and the development of new ones) is a crucial aspect of overcoming the addiction.

To summarize, there is a continuum of repetitive behaviors. At one end lies harmful addiction (costs exceeding benefits); at the other lies positive addiction (benefits exceeding costs). In the middle is plain habit. All involve craving to some degree. We might also describe the continuum as consisting of bad habits, plain habits, and good habits. When I refer to addiction, I will mean a harmful one, in accordance with the working definition above. I will indicate positive addiction or good habit when that is meant.

The same repeated behavior could be a positive addiction, a harmful one, or a habit. Exercise or wine-drinking are two common examples. Cocaine use is another example, if we consider the coca-leaf chewing of millions of South Americans, which is akin to coffee drinking. Possibly any addictive involvement that lies at the severe end of the continuum, for some individuals, could also be found at the other end, in other individuals (although the behaviors associated with these involvements would be dramatically different). Some involvements may in practice tend toward only one end of the continuum (e.g., toothbrushing), but what happens normally can also happen in unusual circumstances or contexts. A cost-benefit analysis of any behavior must take into account its frequency, intensity, context, and other factors.

In short, to understand your addiction, you need to understand your life. This workbook attempts to help you do that.

What Causes Addiction?

This workbook is about overcoming addiction, and about a broader issue: the management of desire. Addiction develops when desire goes unchecked. Desire is a fundamental aspect of human life, and learning to manage desire is part of normal human development. Overcoming addiction is a special case of managing desire. Overcoming addiction is managing desire writ large.

I leave out of this discussion some Eastern approaches to living, in which the goal of proper living is the elimination of desire. In the Western tradition life is about satisfying desire.

Some desires have their own names: hunger, thirst, greed, lust. Otherwise, we speak of desiring (seeking, wanting, wishing for) various objects and situations in our lives. We feel these desires with varying degrees of intensity. We spend our time identifying, sorting and acting on our desires. We attempt to satisfy those reasonably within our reach. We feel lucky when we get something we weren't sure we could obtain and disappointed when we miss out on something we thought was within easy reach.

The stuff of daily life is effort expended to satisfy desire. We work or go to school, possibly because we are satisfied by these activities in themselves, but also because we earn or hope to earn money to purchase items and experiences, to satisfy our desires. We seek satisfaction (we might also call it pleasure). What money buys will bring us satisfaction directly or position us to obtain satisfaction. Besides money making, we engage in many other activities that are means to other ends. Those ends ultimately can be described as satisfaction, or as happiness. There are vast differences in what individuals find satisfying. There are also vast differences in their capacity to accept new satisfactions in place of old. Changing one's satisfactions is central to overcoming addiction.

Conflict is also the stuff of daily life. Conflict occurs when one person desires this, and another desires that (she wants to go to the beach; he wants to go to the mountains), or the same person desires both this and that (two incompatible things). In addiction, for instance, a conflict can occur between a desire for substance-induced euphoria and a desire for health. Recognizing and examining this conflict are the first steps to managing addiction, just as they are for managing other conflicts. Both sides need to "sit at the negotiating table" and air their agendas before resolution can be found. Chapters 3 through 5 describe how to do this for addiction. As I will amplify in Chapter 5, if there is no conflict, there is no addiction. Under certain circumstances what might look like addiction is not addiction, because the conflict does not exist. "Morphine addiction" in the terminal patient is a clear example.

Unlike the aforementioned Eastern approaches, this book focuses on advancing or maturing desire and satisfaction. We can outgrow earlier or excessive pursuits (and the desires that prompt them), by developing equally (even if somewhat differently) satisfying pursuits. At age five my favorite food was popsicles. I still enjoy an occasional popsicle, but my tastes have matured. Freud called the process of reaching higher satisfactions "sublimation." Socrates called it ascending the "ladder of love." In Chapter 11 we discuss higher satisfactions. One goal of this workbook is to transform desire itself. Otherwise we are, in varying degrees, slaves to it.

As a drive state (such as hunger), desire prompts us to do what we need to do to survive. As a craving or want, it motivates us to pursue experiences that lead to pleasure, satisfaction, and at times, euphoria. Without desire we would not survive, nor pursue activities. We would have no reason to. However, desire can be unmanaged or mismanaged. Addiction is one form of this mismanagement. You may judge for yourself the extent to which mismanaged desire, particularly by those in power, has brought suffering upon humankind.

In severe addiction the desires related to satisfaction appear to become confused with the desires related to survival. Over time our satisfactions actually decrease, but we pursue our addictions as if our survival depended on them. Fortunately it is possible to overcome this situation, as described in Chapter 9.

What Is the Scientific Support for This Book?

There is substantial scientific literature on the treatment of addiction. I have not provided references in the text because they are of little immediate value to the individual desiring to overcome addiction. In the annotated bibliography (Appendix B) are several works which can provide a gateway to the scientific and popular addiction literature.

The treatment of activity addictions is largely unstudied, and the treatment of addiction to substances other than alcohol firmly supports at present only one treatment -- methadone maintenance for heroin addiction. More than being a treatment itself, receiving methadone in place of heroin sets the stage for making other improvements.

This leaves treatment for alcohol problems, which fortunately has been well studied. Over 200 randomized controlled clinical trials of various alcohol treatments are now published in the scientific literature. Several treatments have emerged as effective: the community reinforcement approach, behavioral marital therapy, moderation training, brief motivational counseling, social and coping skills training, and aversive conditioning. Some medications and stress management training are also effective. These treatments are neither well known nor widely available. American addiction treatment is almost entirely traditional (disease model and 12-step oriented). This lack of alternatives is one of the reasons this workbook is needed.

This workbook presents an integration of ideas that appear in various forms across all or many of these alcohol treatments: a generic empirically supported treatment for addiction. Fortunately this generic approach appears likely to apply well to activity addictions and other substance addictions. Clinical judgement is certainly involved in the integration proposed here, and other clinicians might have integrated these treatments differently. Nevertheless, I am confident that most empirically oriented addiction clinicians will agree with the main ideas of this workbook.

What Does "Overcoming Addiction" Really Mean?

Although you can't really judge a book by its cover, with the multitude of books in contemporary society, the cover of a book may be all that most individuals read of it. Because "addiction" is often a negative concept, I was initially concerned that many people would pass this book by, thinking "I'm not addicted." How would they discover that the workbook assumes that everyone has had some degree of addiction, probably to multiple substances and activities? How would they discover that the book is potentially beneficial even to someone who is not an "addict" or "alcoholic"? That's where the list of addictions on the page opposite page 1 comes in. My hope is that listing many types of addiction, which cover a wide range of typical severity, helped you realize this book is about everybody.

On the other hand, individuals who have experienced substantial addiction problems may feel that the notion of everyone being addicted trivializes their problems. The daily heroin user and someone who watches too much TV or who eats too much chocolate may not think of themselves as having much in common.

My middle course is to recognize the vast differences between individuals in the consequences they have experienced because of addiction (as well as how they are perceived by society), but to suggest that there are common elements in overcoming addiction. The workbook presents these common elements. For those with less severe addictions the workbook by itself may be sufficient for completing desired changes. If those with severe addictions are not completely helped, then with luck they have made progress.

"Addictive behavior" has replaced addiction in the last two decades for many psychologists, and it is the term I typically use day to day. It seems to fit better with the idea of a continuum of addictive problems, the possibility of either substance or activity addictive behaviors, and the active role of the individual involved. I chose "addiction" as less cumbersome for the printed page. "Habit" is another option. It avoids the immediate negative connotations of addiction. However, the sense of "habit" for most readers may not include the severe addictions, which are definitely a focus of this workbook.

"Overcoming" is part of the title in order to emphasize the possibility of getting completely past addiction. You can so fully overcome addiction that there is nothing special you need to do to stay free of it. You can be finished with it!

To have thoroughly concluded that "I can live without it" is, for the severely addicted, a critical accomplishment. With luck, individuals at any level of addiction can go beyond this discovery, to accomplish the ultimate purpose of overcoming addiction: *to live even better without it.*

How To Use This Workbook

I have attempted to write a brief but comprehensive workbook for overcoming addiction. For some individuals only a relatively brief effort to overcome addiction is needed, and the brevity of this work is appropriate for them. Nevertheless, I have attempted to cover the major issues typically involved. Even if some of these issues are not pertinent for you now, it will be good to be aware of them. They could come up later in your life -- possibly with another addiction.

This workbook covers addiction in general *because overcoming addiction is one process,* and you will probably need that process several times in your life. Most individuals actually have many addictions, of varying degrees of severity, not just one. Even if only one is a significant problem for you now, the others may still be in need of changing later. Changing one large negative behavior usually involves changing many smaller negative behaviors, as well as developing many positive behaviors. If you learn general principles of behavior change, you can apply them as many times as you need to -- for the "big ones," and the not-so-big ones.

Each chapter begins with an *Overview.* The Overviews are also collected together in the *Summary* at the end of the workbook (Appendix A). By reading this Summary you can identify the chapters of most use to you.

The *Questions* and *Projects* at the end of each chapter help you consider how to apply what you have just read. There is lots of space to make notes. Record the ideas and techniques that are most relevant for you.

If you make enough notes, you'll make it your book, because it will cover what you need. Even if you are not writing answers to the Questions and Projects, you may want to read them, because some ideas from the main chapter text are not fully elaborated until then. If you are progressing through the chapters as part of psychotherapy, the Questions are also intended to provide springboards for discussion for you and your therapist.

The process of overcoming addiction is typically not neat or organized. The individual's journey often does not make sense until nearly the end. Although there is in the abstract one process of overcoming addiction, there are as many expressions of this process as there are individuals. The workbook attempts to allow for this variability. In the final section of each chapter you are encouraged to record the ideas of the chapter that are most useful for you at that particular moment. On later readings, which are encouraged, other ideas may be recorded instead. Your notes will become a log of your journey of discovery, a log that will help you make full sense of the journey when it's complete.

Any changes you make in your life are ultimately your own responsibility. They will be made in your own way, and you will deserve full credit for them. There are as many ways to change as there are individuals. Keep trying until you find what works for you. I hope that many of the ideas in this workbook will be helpful to you. If they are not, remember that you can also look elsewhere for guidance. The Bibliography and Resources at the end of the workbook and the support groups listed in Chapter 6 provide places to start. You might also consider (or reconsider) traditional treatment and support groups.

For Whom Is This Book Intended?

Most individuals who overcome addiction will do so with minimal outside assistance. In the professional literature this recovery without professional treatment or support group attendance is called "natural recovery." If you doubt that this is possible, consider smoking. Almost everyone who quits smoking does so without attending treatment or a support group. Perhaps we should not be surprised by this. Everyone knows its easy to quit smoking, right? Wrong! Studies also document natural recovery from alcohol and heroin use.

Treatment for addiction is an adjunct to a naturally occurring process, rather than an essential component of recovery. In medical treatment it is assumed that the patient has a natural capacity for healing. Medical intervention aims to get the patient over one or a few specific obstacles to health, but not all of them.

Many will overcome addiction without the assistance of a workbook. If natural recovery is not occurring, buying and reading a workbook is a smaller step than entering treatment. This workbook may also be a useful adjunct for someone who has sought treatment, especially individual or couples psychotherapy or counseling. The therapist and the client might progress through the workbook together. As noted below, the workbook may not serve well as an adjunct to traditional treatment.

For individuals with severe addictions this workbook can be an introduction to change -- an overview of it. However, the workbook may need to be supplemented with additional readings and professional services. Individuals with severe addictions also typically have multiple and often severe additional problems -- poor health, relationship problems, financial problems, work dysfunction, inadequate social support, depression, an anxiety disorder (phobia, panic, PTSD, generalized anxiety), attention deficit disorder or developmental disorders, major psychiatric or personality disorders, or other problems. Overcoming this set of problems usually involves making improvement on all of them, and significant help is often needed.

There is a range of beliefs about the traditional approach to treatment. If you view it as the only route for your recovery, this workbook probably will not be helpful to you. The differences in approach would probably require so much "translating" as not to be worth the effort.

However, you may view the traditional approach and this alternative as different but equally valuable, at least given what you know about them. If you are not committed to one approach, this workbook may help you make a decision. Most individuals will fare best if they select one approach or the other, because many (although not all) of their ideas are opposites of one another. However, I also believe that there are as many roads to recovery as there are individuals. Regardless of your other choices, I would be pleased if this workbook is useful to you.

Although the underlying ideas in this workbook are also applicable to adolescents, the presentation of these ideas has been done herein with adults in mind. A separate workbook would be needed to present these ideas adequately to adolescents.

Why Am I Qualified to Write This Workbook?

I am a clinical psychologist who started practice in 1984 in San Diego, California. Since 1985, I have specialized in providing "alternative treatment" for addiction. Prior to 1985, I had been aware of the lack of options in American addiction treatment. I have a personal passion for "reason" and the development of reasonable solutions to problems. The 12-step idea that addiction could be resolved *only* by reliance on a "higher power" made no sense to me. I do not doubt that a spiritual awakening can resolve addiction and many other problems, but I do not believe that it is the *only* method that will work. The idea that addiction could be resolved *only* by speaking with others who are "recovering" from addiction also seemed unreasonable.

If I take my broken arm to the emergency room of a Catholic hospital, they treat it using entirely non-spiritual methods. If I ask to see a priest, they willingly send one, but they probably don't suggest I see one either. The hospital's view is: God exists, but we don't need to go that high to repair a broken arm.

Whether the physician setting the arm had previously also had a broken arm is not relevant to his or her ability to set mine. We know enough now about overcoming addiction that a well-trained mental health professional can help someone regardless of the professional's personal history. If you accept the ideas in this workbook, you will also realize that we all have in common some level of personal experience with addiction.

I believe that there might be many different types of spiritual awakenings, not just the type suggested by AA. Addiction treatment needs to be able to accommodate all types of spiritual awakening. I hope that for many readers the exercises suggested by this workbook, particularly those in Chapters 11 and 12, will lead to a type of spiritual awakening or support other spiritual awakenings of the reader's choosing.

In graduate school, I took one course on "alcoholism," but it exclusively focused on 12-step based treatment. Later I discovered that there was a substantial scientific literature on the treatment of addiction, but treatment based on this literature was not widely available. By 1985 I decided that I wanted to make these treatments available for those who preferred them. This workbook summarizes what I have learned by study of addiction and its treatment, and by listening and learning from clients as we work together to apply the sometimes abstract principles of change in their very specific lives.

Although for many of my colleagues working with addiction is decidedly not appealing, I have found it very satisfying. There are significant prejudices against individuals with addiction: "How can you tell when an addict is lying? When his lips are moving." "When an alcoholic tells you how much he drinks, double or triple it if you want the truth." Although there are certainly times when addicted individuals deceive professionals (and sometimes, even more importantly, themselves), deception and self-deception are not unique to addiction. Professionals with negative attitudes toward addiction need to consider the role their own nonempathic, antagonistic or controlling behavior might play in eliciting the behavior they object to. Most individuals with addiction respond well to empathic listening, sincere concern and a flexible perspective. In time most of them make major changes.

But What If You Really Are an Addict (or Alcoholic)?

If your perspective on addiction includes labelling yourself as an "addict" or "alcoholic" who has a disease, then this workbook probably is not for you. AA and other 12-step groups are easy to find because they are listed in every American phonebook. There are over 96,000 AA meetings around the world each week, and additional thousands of other 12-step groups. Many individuals report that their success in overcoming addiction occurred because of the insights and support they received in 12-step groups.

However, if you are not sure that this is your perspective, you may be interested in knowing the following facts. Although many individuals seek out AA (and I recommend attending a meeting if you have never done so), most do not follow through for any significant length of time. As noted above, *the majority of individuals who recover "naturally" do so without attending AA, other 12-step groups, or treatment.* Although there is a very large body of professional writing on AA, it has been infrequently studied with scientific controls, and scientific judgement on its effectiveness cannot yet be made. 12-step based treatment, which helps someone make good use of attending 12-step groups, has only recently been supported by research as possibly being as effective as the proven treatments I mentioned earlier. None of the proven treatments are based on understanding addiction as a disease, nor are they based on a belief in a "higher power" (which is the cornerstone of the AA approach). In the proven treatments addiction is understood as lying on a continuum, and clients are given a range of options about how to participate in treatment and what treatment goals to have.

The traditional approach is the most widespread (if you doubt that just call a few treatment centers listed in your local yellow pages), but there is no need to be embarrassed about pursuing an alternative approach if you desire to do so. You have substantial scientific justification for this choice.

One final note by way of introduction. I suggest that you not use the labels "addict" or "alcoholic." They are examples of all-or-none thinking and may be unhelpful because you can waste effort on wondering whether the label applies to you. You can think of yourself as having had problems (plural) because of the substance or activity, and as now wanting to change your relationship with it. To say you have "a problem" is just to reword addict and alcoholic. This rewording may be some improvement, but you are still thinking in all-or-none terms (some have a problem, some don't). Even the term "addiction" is a convenience for the sake of writing this book. You could use "habit" or any other term you prefer. If you believe that you have had some problems from one or more substances or activities, and if you desire to reduce or eliminate these problems, the pages that follow will show you what to do.

2

Getting Started

Overview

Addiction is excessive involvement, in varying degrees, with any substance or activity. The costs of involvement clearly outweigh the benefits, but involvement continues repeatedly because it is craved. This workbook presents ideas (and techniques) for overcoming addiction which have been helpful to many others. Some ideas may be helpful to you; some may not. Ultimately, you will need to use your own judgement about which ideas to adopt. There are as many ways to overcome addiction as there are individuals. This workbook can be useful if you are ready to overcome addiction now, have overcome it but want to review your work, or are unsure about overcoming addiction and want to consider information about how to do it.

Recognizing Addiction

When this book was introduced at the American Psychological Association Convention in San Francisco in August 1998, one participant saw the title, *Sex, Drugs, Gambling & Chocolate*, and remarked, "All my favorite things!"

You probably are well aware of your primary addictions. I'll assume you have several of them. Check the list of addictions opposite page 1, as there may be more you want to add to your own list! Having more than one addiction is more common than just having one.

You may know people who
⇒ smoke and drink
⇒ smoke and drink too much coffee
⇒ use one drug and also use others
⇒ use drugs and drink
⇒ gamble and drink and overspend
⇒ engage in high-risk sex and drink and use drugs
⇒ are overdependent in a relationship and escape often to fantasy
⇒ overeat and watch too much television.

You probably have struggled with what to do about your own addictions. You may have ignored them for long stretches of time. Now may be the time to take further steps, and this workbook is full of ideas you can use! Just by reading this workbook you are taking a step. I hope that you make significant progress in overcoming your addictions. I also know that it may be some time before you are fully "ready, willing and able" to make complete changes. Even if you are not fully ready yet, you can now be gaining information for future use.

From the traditional point of view about addiction the question is, "Am I or am I not addicted?" If you accept the above definition of addiction, you need to focus on the more complicated questions of "How addicted am I?" and "Is this addicted enough to do something about?"

Nevertheless, you may still be thinking about the questions "Am I an addict?" or "Am I an alcoholic?" Many are surprised to learn that "addict" and "alcoholic" are not official diagnostic terms (although alcoholic was until 1980). The diagnostic criteria that professionals currently use identify substance "abuse" (less severe addiction) or "dependence" (more severe addiction). Incidentally, the criteria for activity addictions are less well developed. The criteria are useful for evaluating an addiction. However, much more detailed criteria are presented in Chapters 3, 4 and 5.

Diagnostic Criteria for Substance Dependence and Substance Abuse

Substance Dependence

A maladaptive pattern of substance use, leading to clinically significant impairment or distress, as manifested by three (or more) of the following, occurring at any time in the same 12-month period:

(1) tolerance, as defined by either of the following:

(a) a need for markedly increased amounts of the substance to achieve intoxication or desired effect

(b) markedly diminished effect with continued use of the same amount of the substance

(2) withdrawal, as manifested by either of the following:

(a) the characteristic withdrawal syndrome for the substance (refer to Criteria A and B of the criteria sets for Withdrawal from the specific substances)

(b) the same (or a closely related) substance is taken to relieve or avoid withdrawal symptoms

(3) the substance is often taken in larger amounts over a longer period than was intended

(4) there is a persistent desire or unsuccessful efforts to cut down or control substance use

(5) a great deal of time is spent in activities necessary to obtain the substance (e.g., visiting multiple doctors or driving long distances), use the substance (e.g., chain-smoking), or recover from its effects

(6) important social, occupational, or recreational activities are given up or reduced because of substance use

(7) the substance use is continued despite knowledge of having a persistent or recurrent physical or psychological problem that is likely to have been caused or exacerbated by the substance (e.g., current cocaine use despite recognition of cocaine-induced depression, or continued drinking despite recognition that an ulcer was made worse by alcohol consumption)

Substance Abuse

A. A maladaptive pattern of substance use leading to clinically significant impairment or distress, as manifested by one (or more) of the following, occurring within a 12-month period:

(1) recurrent substance use resulting in a failure to fulfill major role obligations at work, school, or home (e.g., repeated absences or poor work performance related to substance use; substance-related absences, suspensions, or expulsions from school; neglect of children or household)

(2) recurrent substance use in situations in which it is physically hazardous (e.g., driving an automobile or operating a machine when impaired by substance use)

(3) recurrent substance-related legal problems (e.g., arrests for substance-related disorderly conduct)

(4) continued substance use despite having persistent or recurrent social or interpersonal problems caused or exacerbated by the effects of the substance (e.g., arguments with spouse about consequences of intoxication, physical fights)

B. The symptoms have never met the criteria for Substance Dependence for this class of substance.

Reprinted with permission from the Diagnostic and Statistical Manual of Mental Disorders, *Fourth Edition. Copyright 1994 American Psychiatric Association.*

The diagnostic criteria expand the search from one question (Am I addicted?), to two questions (Am I abusing? Am I dependent?). But I encourage you to consider even broader issues: the various problems addiction has caused you, the degree of each of these problems, and the likelihood of these problems continuing if your behavior remains unchanged.

I encourage these broader questions because you can have noteworthy addiction problems, but still not qualify for a formal diagnosis of abuse or dependence. Resolving these nondiagnosable problems will probably not require readjusting your entire life, but the effort to resolve them is still worthwhile. Of course, the effort is even more worthwhile if your addictions are more serious.

In recognizing addiction, craving is another essential factor. Craving is the desire to engage in the addiction, and the intensity of this desire at times can lead us to think that we are "out of control." Craving will be discussed in detail in Chapters 8, 9 and 10, so we cover here only some basic points.

Imagine the following scenario. You are with a heavy cigarette smoker. You have either once tried cigarettes and didn't like them, or you have never tried cigarettes. The two of you are in a situation--be as creative as you like--in which it is impossible for the smoker to obtain cigarettes. As the hours pass, you know what happens to the smoker. Craving for cigarettes increases. This craving in itself is not harmful. If enough time passes, the craving will actually die away. But in the early hours and days of deprivation, the smoker is clearly affected by the lack of cigarettes. If the two of you can escape, just about the first thing the smoker will do is get cigarettes.

Now you also have been without cigarettes this whole time, but there is no impact on you. You don't crave them. If we put a very light smoker in this imaginary scenario (for example, someone who smokes one or two cigarettes a week), it is likely that this individual's craving will be minimal.

Craving arises out of experience with a substance or activity, and it arises roughly in proportion to the amount of experience. The term craving is another way of saying that you are motivated to experience the substance or activity, that you strongly desire it.

Ironically, although you crave an experience, you don't crave craving. Craving itself is uncomfortable and undesirable, which is how it is motivating. By acting on the craving you make it go away, and at least for a while you feel better in two ways. The craving is gone, and you have experienced the pleasure of your addiction as well.

The typical craving cycle goes like this. It begins with the state of not craving. Then the craving begins and grows until the substance or activity (along with the associated high) is experienced. There is a continued addictive episode until the craving stops, or the episode ends for some other reason. Perhaps there was a decision to stop, or there were no more substances or money or whatever you needed, or you passed out. If craving ends before the episode ends, you may have just kept going out of "force of habit." The cycle begins again later, possibly after a period of rest or recovery if this is needed.

   If someone has been through this cycle many times, often with increasingly negative consequences, it may seem reasonable to others to consider this individual as "out of control." There is more to the story than this (and it will take most of the workbook to tell it), but it is common for individuals who have repeatedly been through this cycle to perceive themselves as out of control or, more simply, "I'm addicted to this!" If this scenario sounds familiar, keep reading!

Trusting Your Own Judgement

I'll assume that the ultimate desired outcome of reading this workbook is a reduction or elimination of the costs associated with your addiction. This reduction or elimination of costs will require a change in your addictive involvement. We will discuss shortly how motivated you are to make changes, but for now you have at least enough motivation to be reading! Changes of involvement with your addiction can include abstaining, moderating, or modifying the circumstances and patterns of your involvement. This workbook can guide you in this process of changing your addictive involvement.

Among the steps presented in this workbook are:
⇒ building and maintaining motivation to change
⇒ connecting with others
⇒ identifying and developing alternative coping methods
⇒ reducing resentment about changing
⇒ identifying, understanding and coping with craving
⇒ developing other satisfactions
⇒ building a new, balanced life
⇒ staying alert for problems and following through all the way

You will need to make decisions about each step, but there is one decision needed just to get started: how much to trust your own judgement. Only you will be able to decide which ideas in this workbook apply to you. You will need to think about each one and try it out, first in imagination, and possibly in practice. Like a scientific researcher, you will need to determine which ideas seem most promising and need to be tested first. Of course, if these early ideas are successful, you may not need to try many more! The whole process, however, will need to be guided by your own judgement.

AA: Powerlessness, social support, and empowerment

Alcoholics Anonymous and other 12-step groups suggest that in order to recover from addiction you must accept that you are powerless to recover on your own. Only with inspiration from a higher power, recognition of your own character defects, and fellowship in the group, among other steps, will you be successful. If this perspective makes sense to you, I encourage you to attend 12-step groups.

AA was established in 1935. Other groups have followed; several hundred types of 12-step groups now exist. These groups have been attended by millions around the world. Many participants report that their success is directly attributable to participation in the groups and acceptance of a higher power in their lives.

I believe that many who have been helped by 12-step groups have benefited primarily from what might be called "social support" (as well as some of the useful behavioral guidance of 12-step groups) rather than from a deep acceptance of the 12-step philosophy. I also believe that some individuals will recover *only* by participating in 12-step groups. I believe there are relatively few of these individuals. Most individuals might benefit from a variety of approaches to change. Unfortunately, there are also individuals who may not significantly benefit from any.

The social support provided by 12-step groups is similar to the support provided by any discussion group of individuals with common problems. In such a group participants can describe their own experiences and express their feelings about them, identify individuals (models) to emulate, realize that however much they have struggled others may have struggled even more, discover alternative solutions for problems they have faced, learn about problems that might occur in the future and ways to solve them, experience the care and concern of others, and momentarily transcend their own problems by caring for others. Regardless of the underlying philosophy of such a group, or even in the absence of a philosophy, these experiences are likely to be therapeutic for most individuals. In physical health care it is recognized that when patients are well connected to others and speak with them regularly, whether it is a support group, friends, family or others, health, well-being and longevity are better. Love is the best drug. Evidence is now emerging that 12-step based treatment may be as helpful as proven treatments. I believe that what is being observed, in most cases, is the power of social support, not the power of the 12 steps.

I believe that for many who attend 12-step groups the result of group participation is, ironically, a sense of empowerment derived from the processes of social support. Consequently, even if you are committed to the alternative perspective presented in this workbook, or some other alternative perspective, you might find 12-step meetings helpful. Few of my clients have attended them regularly, perhaps because in San Diego alternative groups exist (these groups are discussed in Chapter 6). If alternatives are not available in your locality, 12-step groups might be a sensible option for you. They do not conduct a "belief test" at the door. Meetings are generally considered open to anyone who desires to stop drinking or using, so at least abstainers fit in. If you're quiet about your points of disagreement, you might benefit from the social support as well as other aspects of the meeting. You might even leave feeling empowered!

Do you think your judgement is good enough to choose what will be most helpful? Sometimes self-doubt becomes very strong, especially if you have come to think of yourself as "out of control." I suggest, however, that even if you are self-doubting, you still have capabilities and can still make some good decisions, even if you also make not so good ones. As you are reading now, you are still able to identify words and understand them. You have decided to continue reading, which is a good decision because it keeps open the possibility that you will learn something new that could be helpful. The fact that you are reading this workbook indicates that you are searching for information and that you realize that you need new information and perspectives. Half of solving any problem is recognizing it. So you are not completely without judgement, resources or capabilities!

One of the common thinking errors is all-or-none thinking. If you have made some less-than-great decisions (and who hasn't!), then it may seem sensible to conclude that your judgement is completely gone. However, I suggest that this conclusion is an example of all-or-none thinking. Your judgement in many (if not most) areas of your life is fine. You take this competence for granted, but it is nevertheless real. If your judgement is adequate in these areas, you can develop it in other areas also.

I suggest that your judgement is good enough to select the ideas in this workbook that will be helpful and to make progress on overcoming addiction. It may take you more time than others to get where you are going. You may even make more less-than-great decisions along the way. These decisions can be corrected later, because you will have the judgement to see that they need to be improved. You have learned how to do other things in life. You can learn how to overcome addiction.

You might ask, if my judgement is so good, why haven't I overcome addiction sooner? I suggest that the answer is that you haven't focused on it sufficiently. You haven't focused on it because it seemed too difficult. To attempt to overcome addiction involves facing up to the conflict that on the one hand you want it, and on the other you don't want to give it up. Many of us, faced with this kind of conflict, just hope the conflict will go away. If you are unsure about overcoming addiction, there are always other problems you can pay attention to! We do our best, of course, to prioritize our problems, but even individuals with superlative judgement have difficulty doing this. I suggest that *it's not that you couldn't solve the problem, it's that you weren't facing the problem.*

You may also have been mindful of the possibility that the conflict might go away on its own, just as you wished. Changing jobs or neighborhoods, developing new relationships, or other life changes are often associated with addiction changes. We have all seen how these situational changes can bring about improvements. If your addiction helps you cope with the stress of a perfectionistic boss, but you think your boss may be transferred soon, wouldn't it make some sense just to wait?

On the other hand, it may be a long wait. There is also no guarantee that a change in situation will necessarily produce a change in addiction, so you may still need to make an effort.

I suggest that whenever you decide to face up to the addiction, you have the judgement to guide yourself through the process. You are the only person who ultimately can make the needed decisions, and you will make them when you are ready.

Are You Really Willing to Change?

Every project presents its own unique difficulties. Consider writing a book to help others overcome addiction. Should there be a separate book on each addiction? For each common addiction combination? For those who want to moderate and for those who want to abstain? For mild, or moderate or severe addictions? I have answered all of these questions "no." There are lumpers and splitters, and so far I am a lumper.

But there is another kind of splitting I have not addressed yet. Regardless of the severity of their addictions, people are on a wide spectrum of willingness to overcome them. For one person, making an unfortunate remark (after having had a second drink) is enough to decide to stop drinking. For another person, losing home and family because of enslavement to cocaine is not enough to decide to change.

This range of willingness to change has actually been well studied, and levels of willingness have been described. These levels have been termed the "stages of change." The levels were found by comparing individuals who change their addictions (and other problematic behaviors) by themselves, with individuals who got outside help for these same tasks. As it turns out, the levels are the same for both groups (more lumping!):

Precontemplation. Precontemplators do not want to change their addictions. They may not even consider addiction a problem. They are usually unwilling to think much about their addictions.

Contemplation. Contemplators are well aware that a problem exists, and they are seriously considering doing something about it. They devote some time to thinking about what they might do and weigh the costs and benefits of the addiction as well as of different ways to change it.

Determination. During this stage, the individual begins to take small steps toward solving the problem and commits to taking major steps within a month.

Action. This is the stage of major effort and behavior change. It is the most visible of the stages and is defined as lasting from one day to six months of successful action.

Maintenance. This is the "relapse prevention" stage. Short-term success has occurred in the action stage. Now long-term projects are the focus. Progress on them makes a return to the addiction less and less desirable, and less and less likely.

Termination. If between two and five years have gone by without a return to the addiction, and all craving has gone away, it is reasonable to consider the formerly addicted individual as now entirely free of the problem. Similarly, if you have cancer and then show no sign of it for five years, your diagnosis changes from "cancer in remission" to "no diagnosis."

Relapse. Although termination is the desired endpoint of the change process, in reality most individuals cycle through the stages several times before termination occurs. For instance, someone might slip from Maintenance to Contemplation and stay there for a period of time before Action is again engaged in. Fortunately, once someone has made it to Action, it is unlikely that he or she will fall back all the way to Precontemplation.

Back to the problem of how to write a book on helping people overcome addiction. Most of the material available to help individuals overcome addiction is directed toward those in the action stage. However, most addicted individuals are not in the action stage. Information that is immediately relevant in the action stage (such as how to cope with craving) is less relevant in precontemplation and contemplation. Other mismatches between the individual's stage of change and the information presented to that individual can occur. So perhaps there ought to be separate books for each stage?

I don't think so. There are no "pure" members of any stage of change. Everyone has been in these stages multiple times, not only because of multiple addictions, but because of other problematic behaviors (the ideas in this workbook can be useful for these as well). Furthermore, everyone probably is in each of these stages now, for different addictions or other behaviors. Lastly, because of the reality of relapse, you may need at some point to know about each stage.

I have elected to deal with this problem as follows. Chapters 2 to 5 are primarily intended for contemplators. These chapters focus on establishing and enhancing motivation for change. Chapters 6 and 7 address ideas that are most relevant to determination. These ideas are that no one *has* to change, and that if reduction of addiction occurs, other coping behaviors need to be increased. Chapters 8 to 12 focus on action stage issues of coping with cravings, and the development of alternative satisfactions and an alternative lifestyle. Maintenance is addressed by all the chapters, but especially Chapter 13, on following through to prevent relapse.

I present this material as if you are moving through these stages of change as we move through the workbook. However, I recognize that many readers will not advance through the stages that quickly. The workbook can be customized to one's stage by the process of completing the Questions and Projects at the end of each chapter. I assume that you will devote more attention to Questions and Projects in chapters of immediate interest to you.

Regardless of one's stage of change, the entire workbook is relevant to someone who is unfamiliar with the general approach presented here. Even if you are not ready for action activities, it may increase your motivation to try them later if you at least know specifically what they are. The reminder at the end of each chapter to write down the ideas of most interest to you personally will help you review, if you return to the chapter later, how your thinking has developed over time. This reminder section is titled "What's most important now." This is where you can summarize the workbook ideas that are most important *for you, at this time*. What you will write in this section (and the Questions and Projects) will depend in part on your stage of change.

Let me review this again.
⇒ If you are *uninterested in changing* (and simply reading for information), you may make few or no notes.
⇒ If you are *unsure about changing,* your notes will probably focus on the ideas that help you decide what you want to do (especially Chapters 2 to 5) and how you want to do it (the rest of the workbook).
⇒ If you are *ready to change*, you might focus especially on Chapters 6 and 7 (the reality of choice and the need for alternative coping skills and adequate social support). You might also review the rest of the workbook as well, because you need to know where you are going in order to feel confident about beginning. With luck you will decide that change is more achievable than you had previously thought, and you will record the reasons for your optimism.
⇒ If you have *recently started to change*, you might focus on coping with craving and building a new life (Chapters 8 to 12) and make notes about how you will accomplish these tasks.
⇒ If you are *maintaining a change you began awhile ago*, you might focus on following through completely (Chapter 13). You can also review the entire workbook to identify and record relevant ideas you might have missed earlier.

You might read and take notes in this workbook several times, each time with a different focus. Although the *Overview* at the beginning of each chapter is one summary of that chapter's contents, your own notes can summarize what *you* need to concentrate on, at each stage in the process, to overcome your addiction.

You'll need to decide how rigorous you are going to be about writing answers and notes. They can be written out in detail, but they can also be done briefly or in your mind only. How good they look is not important. Identifying helpful ideas and insights into yourself *is* important (and I suggest writing down the crucial ones to prevent forgetting them). As I mentioned earlier, I also suggest that you read the Questions and Projects even if you are not doing them, because ideas from earlier in each chapter are further elaborated there.

Selecting an Addiction or Addictions to Focus On

We have left it open thus far about which addiction or addictions you will contemplate changing. I mentioned earlier that you probably have several. Several questions arise: Should I attempt to overcome all of them at once? Or maybe just a few? Or the biggest or smallest first?

Ironically, this set of questions, which typically is of great interest to many who are overcoming addiction, has been addressed little by research. My clinical experience is clear, however, about what most individuals actually do. Most change is brought on by some form of "crisis." Consequently, initial change efforts are aimed at the addiction, or possibly the cluster of addictions, that have brought on the crisis. For instance, a drunk driving arrest might bring on interest in reducing drinking, but no initial interest in stopping smoking. A doctor's warning about needing to lose weight would probably not also lead to interest in reducing gambling. A relationship crisis might lead one to aim toward being less dependent on the relationship for organizing one's life, but not increase interest in reducing pot smoking.

A crucial question to consider if you are addressing more than one addiction is whether one tends to lead to another, or whether one is used to cope with not having the other. For instance, does smoking lead to having a drink, or does it help you cope with not having a drink? If smoking is a way to cope, then it might not be crucial to address smoking and drinking at the same time. If smoking seems to set the stage for drinking, addressing both simultaneously might be better. Even if drinking is your immediate concern, the way to deal with that concern may include dealing with smoking.

If you select more than one addiction to focus on, many Questions and Projects (at the end of each chapter) will need to be done multiple times, once for each addiction. I suggest not going after all your addictions at once if you have several of them. The mild ones may tend to fade away "on their own" once your severe ones have been dealt with. Focusing on several may be too laborious. You are free to focus on as many as you wish, of course, but a narrower focus may increase your chance of success.

Questions . . .

The Questions below are some of those questions I ask a client as we work together one-on-one. Some could require long answers, especially if you want to clarify and qualify your answers. You might also struggle to find the right words to express yourself. Therefore, you might appreciate a listener (or listeners) able to ask good questions and help you understand yourself. For some readers the best way to answer these questions will be in discussion with a trusted person. Perhaps this person will be a psychotherapist or counselor, but it could also be a nonprofessional who cares about you and whom you trust. Some of the questions might also be discussed in a support group.

Notice that the Questions are sometimes grouped together. It is not necessary to answer each one. Answer the questions most relevant to you. If it would be helpful, rewrite certain questions. This is *your* workbook now. Don't work for it, make it work for you!

1. Our working definition is that addiction is involvement despite costs because of craving. Addictions can be rated according to their costs. The greater the costs of an addiction, the more severe it is. We will get more precise about this in Chapter 5, but for now, as a first estimate, list your addictions according to severity. Getting the rating "right" is not important. If you put an addiction into the moderate category, and later decide it is mild or severe, this is not a problem. The purpose for now is to begin focusing on what you might want to overcome.

Severe (or serious) addictions:

Moderate addictions:

Mild addictions:

Not even mild, but I'd be better off without these also:

2. As a check on yourself, do the same severity rating again, but from the perspective of someone who either lives with you or currently knows you very well. This "check on yourself" is similar to what a scientist would do when considering new findings. (Suppose you believe that the universe will expand forever, but your colleague believes it will stop expanding at some point, then collapse. A third research group reports new data obtained from a space probe. You quickly see how this data supports your opinion, but your colleague quickly sees how the data supports her opinion. If each considers the data from the other's perspective, there may be much to learn.)

　　　　You do not have to agree with the other person's (imagined) ratings. For now just attempt to identify what those ratings would be.

Which person's rating are you estimating?

Severe (or serious) addictions:

Moderate addictions:

Mild addictions:

Not even mild, but I'd be better off without these also:

3. As an additional check, consider a third person's ratings. Options for this third person might include some degree of imagination. If your mother or father don't know much about your daily life now (because they are dead, or far away, or you don't tell them much anymore), imagine that they do know. How would your addictions be rated? Or pick another person who has been deeply interested in you, but is now perhaps more removed from your daily life. Or consider what God or someone who could have access to all information about you might think.

Which person's ratings are you estimating?

Severe (or serious) addictions:

Moderate addictions:

Mild addictions:

Not even mild, but I'd be better off without these also:

4. As a different kind of check, consider craving. Craving is part of the definition of addiction. To what extent do you feel out of control of the addictions that are for you most serious, at least at times? Can you recall specific incidents in which you felt out of control? Can you picture these?

Briefly describe an incident in which you apparently had less than full control of one of your addictions. In describing the incident, consider questions about who, what, when, where, why, how, and how much. How intense was the feeling of being out of control? How long did this feeling last?

Briefly describe a second incident, possibly with a different addiction.

5. I have suggested that you have good enough judgement to take further steps to overcome addiction, and that, unfortunately, you may take for granted your own resources and capabilities for change. Consider the addictions that you once had, and have now fully overcome or at least reduced. You may again want to consult the list of addictions opposite page 1. Remember also that there are many more activities and substances than there is space to list. Also remember that overcoming an addiction does not necessarily mean you have stopped all involvement with it. As long as your involvement does not any longer involve significant negative consequences, you have overcome the addiction. I'll elaborate in Chapter 5 on the various aspects of "significant negative consequences," but for now use the ones you can recall.

Addictions you have fully overcome:

Addictions you have reduced in severity:

6. How did you overcome or reduce these addictions (what changes did you make)? To what extent might these same changes be helpful now?

Which addiction?

What changes did you make?

Which changes might be helpful again?

Which changes were not helpful?

What do these unhelpful changes suggest about what to do or not to do in the future?

7. I have suggested that everyone has addictions. Consider the people you know well. What addictions do they have? How severe are these addictions? I do not mean to suggest that everyone has severe addictions, but I do suggest that it is helpful to realize that you are basically not different from other people in this matter, even if their addictions are less severe than yours.

A person you know well:

This person's addictions and their severity:

Another person you know well:

This person's addictions and their severity:

A third person you know well:

This person's addictions and their severity:

8. Consider the severity of the addictions for the three individuals you just chose. Were these addictions all more severe than yours, all less severe, or a mixture? If you mostly know people whose addictions are worse than yours, you might conclude that your problems are not too bad. If their addictions are milder, you might conclude you are a hopeless case. I hope you will realize that your addictions could be milder than those of others, but still worth overcoming. Similarly, your addictions could be worse, but you might still not be ready to overcome them. Your addictions will definitely be worse or milder than others, depending on whom you compare yourself with. The most important comparison, however, is with yourself. We will return to the questions below several times, but they are so important we cannot start on them too soon.

Where do you *want* to be going in your life?

Where *are* you going?

How far apart are these two paths?

If these paths are different, how big a factor is addiction in keeping them separated?

9. What addiction or cluster of addictions would you like to focus on at this time? This question is *not* asking for a commitment to overcome the addiction(s). Chapters 3, 4 and 5 will help you consider whether this is the time to proceed. This question simply helps you narrow your focus in preparation for those chapters. What addiction or addictions do you want to *consider* overcoming at this time?

What feelings come up when you consider overcoming these addictions?

Projects . . .

The projects at the end of each chapter can help you move forward on actual
behavior change, which is the ultimate goal of a workbook like this one. Projects
may require different lengths of time, and sometimes I will suggest a length.
Pick the length that best fits your situation.

1. So far, I have been assuming that you don't object to lumping substance
addictions and activity addictions together. Later we'll get to some of the other
lumps I have suggested. I acknowledge that there are significant differences in
the *effects* of different addictions. I suggest that overcoming addiction is mostly
the same process (as presented in this workbook), regardless of the specific
addictions you have. One of the fundamental aspects of this process is coping
with craving.

   You have identified several addictions above. Observe the cravings for
each addiction for about a week. What similarities and differences do you
notice? Besides differences in intensity (for instance, on a 0 to 10 scale), are
there any other significant differences?

   If your urges seem minimal, there may be the additional factor that your
addiction is used to *prevent* craving from occurring. This is often true for
smokers and overeaters. If so, you might pass on this question for now and wait
till Chapter 8 for more information on the subject of craving.

Summarize the information you have gained from this project:

2. If you are completing this workbook in discussion with someone else, honesty is a critical issue. If you are completing the workbook on your own, honesty with yourself is a critical issue. It is possible to reveal too much to someone else. I suggest that it is not possible to reveal too much to yourself.

Imagine that you are about to discuss your addiction(s) with someone trusted. Even though significant trust exists, there is usually a legitimate question about just how much you can trust someone, especially if the information to be discussed is highly personal. This project will help you deal with this question.

A. This project can be done in imagination first, then in reality when you wish. If you allow yourself to become highly involved in imaginary experience, it can be quite powerful. One of the ways you can know that you are highly involved in the imaginary experience of conversation is whether the person you are "speaking" to "speaks" back to you. I am not referring here to auditory hallucinations, but to the capacity we have to imagine the responses of others fully enough that it is as if they are speaking to us.

B. Identify the most sensitive issues or events that might come up in your discussion. These issues or events could include various things you have done, things that have been done to you, how you really feel about yourself, a full description of just how serious your addictions have been, the failures you have experienced, or the ongoing failings you believe yourself to have.

C. Pick the *least* sensitive issue from this list. Then divide that issue into parts or steps, so that you can reveal the least sensitive information at first, without having to reveal all the information. For instance, if you are about to describe the negative consequences of your addictions, pick the least severe addiction, and list the negative consequences in order, from least severe to most severe.

D. Reveal the least sensitive information about the least sensitive issue. In other words, you start by revealing important information, but it will be the least sensitive of this important information. Then, "observe" the reactions you get.

E. Are the reactions you get the ones you want to get? The experience of being understood has been well studied by psychotherapists and counselors. As a very simple guideline, I suggest that if you are *feeling* understood, you probably *are* being understood. If so, you may have "found" a good person to reveal even more information to. You can keep giving more information, step by step. The experience of revealing sensitive information, and having it understood, is therapeutic all by itself. This does not mean that your listener will agree with everything you did or everything you believe. The goal, again, is simply to have your perspective understood and acknowledged. This understanding and acknowledgement may allow you to move forward in self-understanding and behavior change. If you realize that you are understood by another, it can help you to stop doubting yourself and move forward with decisions you need to make.

F. When ready, carry out this project in reality, with one or more trusted individuals.

Summarize the information you have gained from this project:

What's Important Now?

(If you date your answers to these questions, the answers over time will become a diary of your growth. It is likely that in future readings of this chapter different ideas will be important to you, reflecting the fact that you are indeed changing)

Which ideas from this chapter are most useful *to you, now*?

How can you put these ideas into action?

How much confidence do you have in your judgement in selecting these ideas as crucial at this time? (Circle a number; 10 is highest confidence)

0   1   2   3   4   5   6   7   8   9   10

3

The Initial Benefits of Addiction

Can one desire too much of a good thing?
--William Shakespeare (1564-1616)
As You Like It, Act IV, Scene i

Overview
When you began your involvement with (what has become) your addiction, you liked the substance or activity enough to stay involved. You would not have continued unless you liked it at first. Initially the costs of involvement were probably minimal. As you continued, the costs got bigger.

Remembering How It Used to Be
Chapters 3 and 4 address one of the important questions you can ask about your addiction: What do I like about it? This chapter considers what you liked about the addiction at first, and Chapter 4 considers what you like (and need) about the addiction now. What you like about the addiction, then and now, is important because it leads to the related question: What needs does the addiction satisfy?

We like any aspect of our lives when that aspect is pleasurable. There is nothing wrong with pleasure in itself. You liked your substance or activity at first, and you returned to it for that reason. If it hadn't been pleasurable, you would have stopped.

Similarly, we will assume that the needs your addictions satisfy are not a problem in themselves. There is nothing wrong with wanting to be relaxed, euphoric, sociable, or confident, to name a few needs addiction might satisfy. There can be problems with the *methods*, such as addiction, that you use to satisfy these needs. To change an addiction, you are looking for less costly (and better) ways to satisfy these needs. If you don't find other ways to satisfy these needs, you will quite possibly stay involved with the addiction. If you don't understand the needs to start with, you won't be able to find alternative ways to satisfy them.

For instance, gambling in order to relieve boredom does not mean that relieving boredom is bad, only that gambling can be a very expensive way of doing it. Once you know that relieving boredom is an important benefit of gambling (for you), you can set out to find other ways to achieve that benefit. We discuss how to find alternative ways of satisfying needs in Chapter 6.

What you liked about the addiction at first is probably different from what you like about it now. The greater the difference, the more helpful recognizing it will be to your motivation for change ("I just don't get what I used to from this anymore"). However, many of the satisfactions you got at first may still be continuing, at least in some ways. There is more to the story than this, though, because the costs of addiction have been increasing also. We'll cover costs in Chapter 5.

How do I know that the costs of your addiction have been increasing? If they hadn't, you wouldn't be considering a change in your involvement, and you wouldn't be reading this workbook! Possibly, of course, you are reading this book not for yourself, but for someone else. Still, that individual's costs have increased, or *you* wouldn't be reading now.

Each addiction has its own cost-benefit analysis, and this is what we will focus on in Chapters 3 through 5. To prepare for examining the benefits of your addiction, let's consider a simple illustration of how different a cost-benefit analysis can be for different individuals. Imagine one-hundred individuals of roughly your age, sex and background. Survey them about their experiences with any particular substance or activity you choose. To keep this simple, let's imagine that you are interested in their alcohol experiences. Here is what you'll find:

1) Some have not even tried alcohol, or tried so little (a sip or two) that they really have little knowledge of it.
2) Some have tried alcohol sufficiently to have an opinion, which is that they like it so little that they either gave it up or rarely drink.
3) Some like alcohol enough to have it occasionally, but they don't like it enough to have it regularly.
4) Some like alcohol enough to drink regularly, but there doesn't seem to be any evidence of significant negative consequences.
5) Some drink regularly, probably too regularly and too much, because the costs of drinking, though not major, are evident.
6) Some clearly drink too much, because the negatives of their drinking clearly outweigh the positives.

I am doing more lumping here, and there are problems with the lumps I have chosen. What about individuals who have cut back or stopped because of previous problems, or for other reasons? What about individuals who seem to fall between two groups? What about individuals who seem to fit two groups, like someone who drinks rarely, but when drinking has devastating consequences? We are also ignoring, in Groups 4, 5 and 6, whether the alcohol experience accumulated gradually or was love at first sight. All of the these possibilities point to how many complexities a classification system might need to consider. For now, however, ignore these issues, and assume that drinking experiences can be classified along this simple continuum, with little to no experience of alcohol at one end, and too much experience at the other.

Of the one-hundred individuals, how many fall into each of the six groups suggested above? To use very round numbers, we know that about 20% of the U.S. population abstains from alcohol (group 1), about 10% have significant problems (group 6), 15% have some problems (group 5), and the rest (over half) fall into groups 2, 3 and 4.

For other substances or activities that are not, like alcohol, mainstream aspects of society (such as heroin, cocaine, or promiscuous sex), much less is known. However, we can be confident that the percentage of abstainers is much higher, in part because many people are unwilling to try these behaviors even once. When there are more abstainers, there are of necessity fewer people in the other categories. Cigarettes, by comparison, have very few people in groups 2, 3, 4 or 5. Typically, people either are smokers (and in Group 6), or they are not.

One obvious point to this illustration is that the substance (or activity) in itself does not cause addiction. If it did, everyone one who tried alcohol would over time be drawn into group 6. Related to this point is that categories 2 and 3 actually exist, even though many individuals in 4, 5 and 6 have a hard time believing it. The existence of 2 and 3 means that many people don't really enjoy alcohol enough to get into trouble with it. Not only does alcohol by itself not cause alcohol addiction, it doesn't even cause much alcohol pleasure in many individuals. If alcohol doesn't cause much pleasure for someone, that individual naturally does not seek out much alcohol experience.

Let me expand this idea to addiction in general. I am suggesting that for many or even most individuals, even *if* they are willing to be exposed to some substance or activity, enjoyment may be small or nonexistent. Involvement may even be unpleasant (they hate cigarette smoke, alcohol makes them sleepy, pot makes them irritable, coke makes them paranoid, ice cream hurts their teeth, sex with a relative stranger would be too embarrassing, casinos are too noisy and smoky, etc.). Their risk of addiction, to that substance or activity, is zero or close to zero.

Consider the addictions listed opposite page 1. There are some individuals who may enjoy many of them, but I suggest that most individuals will only have a few of significant interest to them. This is a crucial point because it is easier to think "I am addicted to one or a few" versus "I am addicted to everything." Think not only of yourself and the substances or activities that you can easily pass up, but also individuals you know well. Many can, without any great effort, say no to chocolate, but not tobacco; say no to lottery tickets, but not alcohol; say no to pot, but not pills; the examples are nearly endless.

But what if you *do* think of yourself as addicted to everything? I suggest that on examination you will discover a limit to what you are addicted to. You wouldn't have the time to be addicted to everything! Nevertheless, you may have a relatively large number of addictions. What this indicates is that you probably also have other substantial problems, and that addiction is intertwined with them. Overcoming addiction will involve making improvement on these problems also. To put it another way, other problems help give rise to needs that the addiction satisfies.

Addiction is almost always symptomatic of other problems. As addiction is more severe (or there are many addictions), then the underlying problems are also more severe. The flip side is that addiction causes many problems. Therefore, addiction needs to be worked on from both sides: solve the problems that lead to addiction, and overcome the addiction so you won't have so many problems. It may be tempting to blame all one's misbehavior on addiction ("I couldn't help it, I'm addicted!"), and there is even some social reinforcement for this perspective. In reality addiction goes hand in hand with other problems. These problems may not provide us as socially acceptable a rationale for our behavior ("I couldn't help it, I'm selfish!").

Groups 1 and 2 are also noteworthy because they contain individuals with many different reasons for not getting involved with alcohol. These reasons can be in force even if they find alcohol pleasurable. Religious, economic, social, medical, practical, or moral reasons could be involved in decisions not to have alcohol experiences. These reasons may also keep people in groups 2, 3 and 4 from advancing to groups 5 and 6.

To summarize, pleasure from a substance or activity is essential for initial involvement with it. Involvement can grow into need satisfaction (addiction solves problems). It takes more than pleasure to get to groups 5 and 6. Addiction also causes problems. Various reasons can prevent people from experiencing the pleasure of addiction or developing a reliance on it. These same reasons can be used to overcome addiction, regardless of how pleasurable it is.

In Chapter 3 we are focused primarily on the initial pleasures of your involvement. In Chapter 4 we focus more on the purposes the addiction serves, the problems it solves, the needs it satisfies. The questions in each case are the same, but the answers are likely to be different, because over time a relationship with an addiction changes.

There is an exception to the idea of addiction being fun from the beginning, which is that if you are in pain, then anything that gets you out of pain doesn't have to be pleasurable to be desirable. Just getting you out of pain is enough. The pain could be physical or emotional. If this is true for you, only some of the Questions at the end of this chapter may apply to you. But it's worth looking at all of them, as there might have been more benefits to your involvement than you had realized.

Negative Consequences Were Small at First, Then Increased
Probably the negative consequences of your addiction did not occur immediately, or did not occur in a strong way. After all, if the first time you did something new it caused horrible problems for you, would you be likely to go back and try it again?

If the benefits of your addictive involvement at first were substantial, and the negative consequences were minimal or nonexistent, then at first you were experiencing a positive addiction, as discussed in the Introduction. If this situation had only continued!

Resolving Ambivalence

To accomplish something, two basic elements are required. We need to want to accomplish it, and we need to know how to accomplish it. In overcoming addiction, the main issue is wanting to change. The mechanics of changing addiction are not minor, but they are typically less important than the continued commitment to making the change.

In Chapters 3, 4 and 5 we address this fundamental issue of wanting to change. This issue can be difficult because you are really "of two minds" about change: you love the pleasure of the addiction and what the addiction does for you, but you also hate the trouble the addiction causes you. In short, you are ambivalent about changing. If you weren't ambivalent, you wouldn't be reading this workbook. You would either not consider your behavior a problem, or you would have changed already. Again, it's not hard to change a behavior that only causes pain. It's hard to change your addiction because it causes both satisfaction and pain.

What you really want, of course, is to keep the satisfaction but eliminate the pain. If too much of a good thing is causing problems, then maybe by cutting back, or doing something else differently, you could keep the satisfaction but eliminate (or at least greatly reduce) the pain. The traditional wisdom is that cutting back or moderating is impossible once you have become an "addict" or "alcoholic." We'll get into that issue in Chapter 7.

For now, the important question is whether the pain is great enough to do *something*, regardless of whether that is to stop altogether or cut back. As with a conflict between two parties, the place to start is to get your two minds (the one that likes the addiction, and the one that hates the consequences of the addiction) communicating with each other.

Fortunately, you have already lived a number of years and resolved many other ambivalences in life. In many important ways, resolving this ambivalence about your addiction is no different. You have resolved ambivalence before; you can do it again!

Questions . . .

As mentioned before, you may have several addictions to focus on, and if so will need to answer these questions separately for each. *You can duplicate the "Questions" pages for this purpose,* or answer for each addiction on separate sheets of paper, or for some questions divide these pages into columns with one or more vertical lines, or use different color pens/pencils for different addictions.

In these Questions we begin by activating significant memories about your addiction. One analogy for how the mind works is a desk and filing cabinet. In order to work on the contents of a file folder, the folder needs to be on your desk. We could also consider having a tool, but not being able to use it unless it is on or near your workbench, or having software, and needing to have it open (in a multi-tasking environment) in order to use it.

At times I have tried to work on something, oblivious to the fact that the necessary information, or papers, or tools, were out of my sight (and therefore out of my mind). I didn't get very far! We will begin by recalling significant addiction memories, in order to get them onto your work area.

Do not be alarmed if you experience a craving to engage in the addiction. This would be normal, because you are activating pleasant memories of your addiction. If a craving does occur, it's a sign that your activation is strongly occurring. This is good, because it will allow you more access to critical information about your addiction.

To foreshadow information covered in Chapters 8, 9 and 10, if you do experience a craving, it does not mean that you have to act on it. Just continue staying focused on this workbook, and the craving will go away.

1. Recall your very first experience with (what has become) your addiction. Describe what happened, and focus in particular on what seemed enjoyable, pleasurable, interesting and satisfying about this experience.

2. Recall your second experience with this addiction. Describe what happened, and focus in particular on what seemed enjoyable, pleasurable, interesting and satisfying about this experience.

3. Recall your third experience with this addiction. Describe what happened, and focus in particular on what seemed enjoyable, pleasurable, interesting and satisfying about this experience.

4. Recall any other early experiences with this addiction, ones which happened before you began to think of yourself as someone regularly involved with this addiction. In other words, identify any other experiences which might have helped persuade you that this substance or activity was pleasurable, and possibly valuable. Describe what happened, and focus in particular on what seemed enjoyable, pleasurable, interesting and satisfying about this experience.

5. How many experiences with the substance or activity occurred before it became regular (before you considered it a habit)? How long did this take? Were there any points at which you considered it a positive addiction?

6. The experiences described above can help you answer the critical question of this chapter: what did you like about this addiction at first? The checklist below will help you make sure that you have considered the full range of pleasures and satisfactions possible from the addictive experience. You will see an almost identical list of reminders at the end of Chapter 4, where we will look at them as possibly applying to your current experience of the addiction. For now, we are focused on your early experience.

Note that this checklist does not distinguish between pleasures given and needs satisfied. I have suggested that it was pleasure that got you interested in the addiction, but need satisfaction that kept you going with it. However, it can be difficult, and actually unnecessary, to distinguish between pleasure and need satisfaction precisely. Many of the items on the checklist can be thought of as having a component of both pleasure and need satisfaction. The important issue is not to miss either of them as you begin conducting your personal cost-benefit analysis of this addiction.

     I have divided these benefits into categories, but there is some overlap between the categories. Depending on how you experience a particular benefit, you might even consider it as belonging in another category. The categories are not important and are placed here only because they might help you to identify commonalities across your benefits. Ignore the categories if they are distracting.

     It may be tempting to consider your benefits from the perspective of what you *hoped* to achieve from your addiction. However, be as honest with yourself as you can, and identify the benefits you *actually* obtained. If there has been a discrepancy between what you hoped to get and what you actually got, this would be a good time to identify this discrepancy.

     On the list below check off each benefit that applies to your *early* involvement with this addiction. Place three checkmarks if the benefit strongly applied, one checkmark if the benefit was noticeable but not very strong or regular, and two checkmarks if it was in between.

     Then, in the space below each checked item, write a brief reminder to yourself of one or more examples of experiencing that benefit.

My addiction enabled me to obtain the following benefits:

A) Emotional benefits (negative emotions)

___To cope with fear and anxiety
"It helped me cope with feelings like anxiety, tension, fear, stress, agitation, nervousness, vulnerability, intimidation, embarrassment or panic."

___To cope with sadness and depression
"It helped me cope with feelings like depression, sadness, hurt, discouragement, grief, feeling defeated, feeling deprived or feeling abandoned."

___To cope with anger
"It helped me cope with feelings like frustration, resentment, anger, annoyance, irritability or rage."

___To cope with shame or guilt
"It helped me cope with feelings like remorse, being ashamed, or feeling guilty or responsible. The bad things I did didn't bother me as much."

____To cope with disgust or distaste

"It helped me cope with being disgusted by something or finding something distasteful. I was able to overcome my disgust."

____To cope with boredom

"It helped me cope with feeling bored, apathetic, or impatient. I needed it to feel stimulated."

____To cope with overexcitement

"It helped me cope with being too excited. It helped me not act on sexual excitement or not act on other impulses."

____To cope with emotional exhaustion

"It helped me cope when I felt like I had nothing left inside of me."

____To eliminate or reduce a sense of separateness or aloneness

"I didn't feel alone; it was always there when I needed it."

____To cope with a general feeling of emotional pain

"I don't understand why, but I felt tremendous pain, and when I did this the pain was less."

____To cope with other negative feelings

"It helped me cope with loneliness, envy, suspiciousness, alienation, humiliation, shock, feeling powerless or other negative feelings."

____To stabilize my feelings

"It helped me bring my feelings into a more normal range. They were just too out of control without it."

B) Emotional benefits (positive emotions)

___To enhance positive emotional states
"When I felt good, it made me feel even better."

___To feel self-confident or worthwhile
"The only time I really felt good about myself was when I did this."

___To have a pleasurable experience
"This was one of the best ways I knew of to have fun and enjoy myself."

___To experience euphoria
"The high was the best and most enjoyable part of my life."

___To feel fully alive
"I just felt dead or not really alive unless I did this."

C) Social benefits

___To respond to social pressure to engage in the addiction
"When others put pressure on me, it was just easier to do it."

___To improve my social ability
"I didn't know how to enjoy myself with others unless I did this. I could go on a date more easily."

___To experience belonging to a group
"When I did this with my crowd, I knew that I was with them, that I was one of them."

___To cope with feeling socially awkward
"When I did this, I didn't feel insecure, bashful, shy, ill at ease, inadequate, or left out."

___To fit in
"By doing it, I could be involved with others I would not have been able to be involved with, because they wouldn't have accepted me."

___To feel important
"By doing it, I felt that I was important and special; I was somebody.*"*

___To respond to conflict with others
"This was a way to deal with the conflict I had with someone. I couldn't cope with that individual (or group) very well otherwise."

___To rebel
"By doing this, I could show others that I do what I want to do, not what others want me to do."

___To escape from my children
"They could have driven me crazy otherwise!"

D) Physical benefits

___To prevent or reduce physical pain
"It helped me cope with my pain (headaches, arthritis, injuries, surgical complications, chronic illness, or other physical pain)."

___To cope with craving
"It made the craving go away."

___To give me energy to get things done
"I needed it to do what I wanted (or needed) to do."

___To enjoy sex more
"Once I started doing it, sex just didn't seem as good without it."

___To sleep better
"I couldn't get to sleep without it."

E) Intellectual benefits

___To be more creative
"I don't think I could have created what I wanted to without doing this."

___To think better (or more clearly)
"I could be aware of my thoughts better. They were clearer, not too fast and not too slow, and I could follow them more easily."

___To make painful memories go away
"I can't stand remembering those things, and when I did, it made the memories go away."

F) Other benefits

___To test my self-control
"It gave me a chance to see how much I could handle."

___To have activity in my life
"If I hadn't done this, what else would I have done?"

G) Benefits not mentioned

___To experience other benefits not yet mentioned. Although many specific benefits of addiction are listed above, it is impossible to list all of them, or to list each benefit in its varying degrees of intensity. List here any other benefits you experienced during your early involvement with this addiction, and describe them as specifically as you can:

7. Review your checkmarks above. The items with three checkmarks were the primary benefits, for you, of this addiction, during your early involvement with it. Make any revisions that now seem appropriate. For instance, an item that has two checkmarks may now seem like it merits one or three checkmarks.

8. Do these benefits (all the items checked above) seem worthwhile to you? Do they seem like real and legitimate reasons to engage in your addiction? Can you identity any reasons why these benefits would not have been valuable to you? (To repeat an earlier point, I am suggesting that the needs your addiction satisfies are fine in themselves, but the side effects of satisfying these needs with the addiction call into question whether to continue the addiction. It is not the needs that are the problem, but your method of satisfying them.)

9. Summarize in your own words what the benefits of your addiction were, during your early involvement:

Projects . . .

1. As a further aid in activating your memories of your early involvement with your addiction, spend time with any reminders that you have of yourself from that period. You may have photo albums or video tapes of that period. You may

be able to speak with individuals you spent time with then (they may or may not have joined you in the addiction). Try to recall as vividly as possible what was happening in your life, how you were feeling, what was important to you, what your goals were, what your other satisfactions were, and any other aspects of your life that you can recall.

By recalling vividly your life at that time, you may be able to deepen your understanding of how and why the addiction took hold at that time. We are assuming that by getting involved with the addiction you were trying to do something pleasurable and good for yourself. The more you understand what you were trying to accomplish then (even if it wasn't happening very deliberately), the more easily you will be able to find alternative ways to accomplish it now.

Summarize the information you have gained from this project.

What's Important Now?

If you date your answers to these questions, the answers over time will become a diary of your growth. It is likely that in future readings of this chapter different ideas will be important to you, reflecting the fact that you are indeed changing.

Which ideas from this chapter are most useful *to you, now*?

How can you put these ideas into action?

How much confidence do you have in your judgement in selecting these ideas as crucial at this time? (Circle a number; 10 is highest confidence)

0   1   2   3   4   5   6   7   8   9   10

Notes

The Current Benefits of Addiction

4

*When they used to tell me I'd shorten my life ten years
by smoking, they little knew the devotee they were
wasting their puerile words upon -- they little knew
how trivial and valueless I would regard a decade that
had no smoking in it!*
> --Mark Twain (1835-1910)
> Letter to Reverend Joseph H. Twichell
> December 19, 1870

Overview

Because your initial involvement with your addiction was positive, you stayed
involved long enough to develop a habit (a pattern of regular involvement with
costs and benefits about equal) and eventually an addiction. Over time you came
to rely on this habit or addiction as a means of coping with other problems. The
addiction may now be your preferred way to cope with one or more problems.
The effectiveness of your addiction as a coping method may have diminished, but
you may not have realized this.

Your Addiction is a Coping Method

It is possible that the primary or sole factor in maintaining your addiction is
pleasure. Life without the addiction could seem boring, and the addiction
relieves that boredom. However, probably over time you have also come to rely
on the addiction to satisfy other needs and solve other problems. You may be
only partly aware of this aspect of your addiction.

I suggest that there are four phases to the development of an addiction: 1)
curiosity, 2) expected enjoyment, 3) addiction as a coping method, and 4)
addiction as a way of life. If you did not have some initial curiosity, you

51

wouldn't have tried it. If there had not been pleasure, you would not have stayed with it. If the addiction did not also satisfy one or more needs, you wouldn't have become overinvolved with it. If you stay overinvolved with it long enough, the addiction becomes a way of life, and staying involved with it is, among other benefits, a way to have a sense of normality.

Suggesting that there are stages to addiction may lead you to assume that if you are in stage 1 or 2, you will necessarily progress to stages 3 and 4. However, this will not always happen. Stage 2 corresponds roughly to groups 3 and 4, mentioned at the beginning of Chapter 3. As I defined those groups, the individuals in them did not necessarily progress to higher groups. They enjoyed their involvement with a potentially addictive activity, but their involvement was limited and the benefits were not exceeding the costs.

If you were in stage 1 or 2 above, you would not be reading now. If you are in stage 3 or 4, I hope that the idea of these four stages will be helpful to you in understanding the degree to which you have surrendered yourself to addiction. Armed with this understanding perhaps you will be in better position to escape.

Progression in Addiction

It can be easy to confuse mild addiction problems with "early stage" problems. Let's use alcohol as an example. If an individual is "diagnosed" as an "early stage alcoholic," it implies that later stages will necessarily be reached. The "fact" that the individual is an "early stage alcoholic" can then be used to justify restrictions on the individual or treatments that might indeed be appropriate for an individual with severe problems (a "late stage alcoholic"), but which are probably not appropriate for this individual with mild problems.

Most individuals do not "progress" in their addictive involvement all the way to severe problems. Although the negative consequences of the addiction may build up over time, usually they do not. The addictive involvement itself is often fairly steady. Smokers typically don't keep smoking more and more cigarettes. Overeaters don't typically keep gaining more and more weight. Substance users usually get to a steady level and stay there. The American emphasis on severe addiction obscures the fact that most addiction problems are mild or moderate. These addictions occur in people we already know. We just don't think of them as addicted.

Of course, a significant portion (but still well under half) of those with addiction do progress. Someone can also be steady for a long time and then progress. But progression is not inevitable. The primary reason to overcome addiction is not to prevent progression which might happen, but to stop the negative consequences that already are happening. If the intensity of the response to the addiction is based not on what might happen, but what is currently happening, there is much less risk of going beyond what is needed.

In stage 4 addiction we surrender many aspects of life to the addiction, until finally life is almost entirely oriented around it. I want to celebrate: time for the addiction. I am upset: time for the addiction. I am lonely: time for the addiction. I am getting together with others: time for the addiction.

To be sure, not every aspect of life is surrendered to addiction. Some addictions are typically much less social than others, so socializing goes on relatively unchanged. Some addictions may not easily be engaged in every day, so other daily activities continue. However, in severe cases of addiction, there can be an amazing degree of intertwinement between the addiction and the rest of daily living. Think of the smoker who cannot begin anything or go anywhere without having a cigarette before, during and after.

Whether you think of your addiction as a coping method (stage 3) or as a way of life (stage 4), your task at this point is the same, to identify how the addiction helps you cope. If you are in stage 4, you will probably have more needs to identify and develop alternative coping methods for. You may also need to face up to your (irrational) fear that without your addiction you cannot survive. We will address addiction as survival in Chapter 9.

Your Addiction May Not Be Working So Well Anymore

Depending on how long you have been involved with the addiction, it may actually be letting you down. One of the ironies of addiction is that over time it tends to take away from you what it gave you at first, especially if your involvement is progressing. It does not take it away entirely, or, to repeat this point, you probably would have stopped the addiction. If addiction becomes an entirely miserable experience, most individuals give it up. It is because the addiction continues to provide some benefit that it is continued. But consider whether you are now actually worse off than when you began, in precisely the areas you thought you were being benefited.

For example, if the addiction helped relax you before, you may be more agitated than ever. If it gave you energy, you may be more exhausted than ever. If it helped you socialize, you may be more isolated than ever. However, you may not have realized this change. One of the reasons to compare initial benefits and current benefits of your addiction is to identify this change. Of course, when we also consider the rising costs, in Chapter 5, the picture gets even clearer.

If the benefits of your addiction have not diminished, in time they can, particularly with higher involvement, regardless of whether the costs increase. Exactly why this is true is not clear, but undoubtedly it is partly physiological. Considering the (fewer) benefits experienced by individuals with greater addictive involvement than yours may clarify this point.

Rewarding Yourself for Success

As you look ahead to overcoming your addiction, one of your concerns may be that you will be missing out on the benefits of addiction. Although this concern misses the "big picture" that your life will (eventually) be better without addiction, it is often helpful in the early stages of change to establish some (immediate) rewards for changing. The actual benefits of change may be slow in arriving, and we are most influenced by immediate consequences.

In Chapter 7 I will discuss modifying your environment in order to prevent certain behaviors. Rewards influence behavior by coming after it (just as punishments do), establishing expectations about what will happen in the future. The farther away a reward or punishment is expected to occur, the less influence it tends to have over current behavior, because other more immediate consequences are more in mind. For instance, you may realize that there is a good chance you will develop life-shortening disorders if you continue to smoke. However, these disorders may not develop for decades, and the satisfaction of smoking can be experienced immediately. Even though a longer life is probably more important to you than the brief satisfaction of a cigarette (if you were choosing between them at the same time), the brief satisfaction often wins out because it is immediate.

By establishing rewards for yourself, you are bringing the long-term rewards of change into the present, where they can have more influence. Establishing rewards is a way the foresightful part of you can influence the parts of you that can't look that far ahead. Here are several ways to do this:

Praise yourself for any progress that occurs. A simple acknowledgement to yourself (silently, under your breath or out loud: "not bad! I did it! good job! way to go!") can feel good, and make you look forward to hearing the next one.

Encourage (selected) others to praise you. It is good to know that change is being observed and appreciated by others. You may need to talk with them about how to do this. Praise can be overdone, either in its frequency or wording. Simple occasional comments, often just a statement of observable facts, are best: "You went all day with only five cigarettes and only got briefly irritable twice. That's a big improvement from yesterday."

Plan rewards for small steps that you accomplish on the way. Like the punishment that is far away, the big reward that is far away may not have as much influence as the smaller but immediate reward. Especially at the beginning of change, plan to reward yourself frequently for the small steps of change. At first you might reward yourself every time you don't act on a craving. You can taper off these rewards as the natural positive consequences of change begin to occur. In addition to rewards that occur every time a desirable behavior occurs, you might also consider hourly and daily rewards, gradually lengthening to weekly or monthly ones. Examples include doing something special for yourself at the end of a successful day, taking five minutes each successful hour to relax or do something enjoyable, or putting money into an "account" for yourself, for every period of success, to spend on something you truly want.

Questions . . .

As in Chapter 3, we begin by activating significant memories of your addiction. However, we focus here on the current time period, not the time of your initial involvement. You will need to decide whether "current" includes recent weeks, months or years. "Current" could be the period since you began considering the addiction a problem, or since your involvement stabilized at some plateau, or since a relevant significant event occurred (e.g., your partner left you because of the addiction).

As before, do not be alarmed if you experience a craving to engage in the addiction. Just continue staying focused on this workbook, and the craving will go away.

1. Recall a recent experience with this addiction. Describe what happened. Focus on what seemed enjoyable, pleasurable, interesting and satisfying about this experience. Also identify any problems that the addiction helped you cope with.

2. Recall another recent experience with this addiction. Describe what happened. Focus on what seemed enjoyable, pleasurable, interesting and satisfying about this experience. Also identify any problems that the addiction helped you cope with.

3. Recall another recent experience with this addiction. Describe what happened. Focus on what seemed enjoyable, pleasurable, interesting and satisfying about this experience. Also identify any problems that the addiction helped you cope with.

4. If recalling additional experiences seems potentially helpful, describe these as well.

5. Describe your pattern of involvement with this addiction: how much, how often, and the typical people, places, times or events that the addiction is associated with. How stable is this pattern? How fast has it been progressing to higher levels of involvement?

6. As you prepare to consider the checklist below, consider some additional general questions, which may help activate other relevant memories:

What would be hard for you to do if you didn't have the addiction?

What would you miss out on if you didn't have the addiction?

What advantages do you have over people who don't have this addiction?

7. The experiences described above can help you answer the critical questions of this chapter: What do you like about this addiction now? What needs does the addiction satisfy? The checklist below will help you make sure that you have considered the full range of pleasures and satisfactions possible from the addictive experience. Items that were not included in the Chapter 3 checklist, because they are not typically relevant to addiction in its earlier stages, have been indicated as (NEW).

      The categories of benefits (e.g., emotional benefits, social benefits) are not important and are placed here only because they might help you to identify commonalities across your benefits. What is most important is not to miss any benefits. Ignore the categories if they are distracting.

      It may be tempting to consider your benefits from the perspective of what you *hope* to achieve from your addiction. Also, it may be easy to confuse what you first got from the addiction with what you get now. However, be as honest with yourself as you can, and identify the benefits you *actually* obtain *currently*.

If there is a discrepancy between what you hope to get, and what you actually get this would be a good time to identify this discrepancy.

On the list below check off each benefit that applies to your *current* involvement with this addiction. Place three checkmarks if the benefit strongly applies, one checkmark if the item is noticeable but not very strong or regular, and two checkmarks if it is in between.

Then, in the space below each checked item, write a brief reminder to yourself of one or more examples of experiencing that benefit.

My addiction enables me:

A) Emotional benefits (negative emotions)

___To cope with fear and anxiety
"It helps me cope with feelings like anxiety, tension, fear, stress, agitation, nervousness, vulnerability, intimidation, embarrassment or panic."

___To cope with sadness and depression
"It helps me cope with feelings like depression, sadness, hurt, discouragement, grief, feeling defeated, feeling deprived or feeling abandoned."

___To cope with anger
"It helps me cope with feelings like frustration, resentment, anger, annoyance, irritability or rage."

___To cope with shame or guilt
"It helps me cope with feelings like remorse, being ashamed, or feeling guilty or responsible. The bad things I did don't bother me as much."

___To cope with disgust or distaste
"It helps me cope with feelings like being disgusted by something or finding something distasteful. I am able to overcome my disgust."

___To cope with boredom
"It helps me cope with feeling bored, apathetic, or impatient. I need it to feel stimulated."

___To cope with overexcitement
"It helps me cope with being too excited. It helps me not act on sexual excitement or not act on other impulses."

___To cope with emotional exhaustion
"It helps me cope when I feel like I have nothing left inside of me."

___To eliminate or reduce a sense of separateness or aloneness
"I don't feel alone; it is always there when I need it."

___To cope with a general feeling of emotional pain
"I don't understand why, but I feel tremendous pain, and when I do this, it is less."

___To cope with other negative feelings
"It helps me cope with loneliness, envy, suspiciousness, alienation, humiliation, shock, feeling powerless or other negative feelings."

___To stabilize my feelings
"It helps me bring my feelings into a more normal range. They are just too out of control without it."

B) Emotional benefits (positive emotions)

___To enhance positive emotional states
"When I feel good, it makes me feel even better."

___To feel self-confident or worthwhile
"The only time I really feel good about myself is when I do this."

___To have a pleasurable experience
"This is one of the best ways I know of to have fun and enjoy myself."

___To experience euphoria
"The high is the best and most enjoyable part of my life."

___To feel fully alive
"I just feel dead or not really alive unless I do this."

___To experience being normal (NEW)
"I need to do this in order to feel normal. Otherwise my life feels wrong, out of whack, strange."

C) Social benefits

___To respond to social pressure to engage in the addiction
"When others put pressure on me, it is just easier to do it."

___To improve my social ability
"I don't know how to enjoy myself with others unless I do this."
I can go on a date more easily."

___To experience belonging to a group
"When I do this with my crowd, I know that I am with them, that I am one of them."

___To cope with feeling socially awkward
"When I do this, I don't feel insecure, bashful, shy, ill at ease, inadequate, or left out."

___To fit in
"By doing, it I am involved with others I would not be able to be involved with as much, because they wouldn't accept me as much."

___To feel important
"By doing it, I feel that I am important and special; I am somebody."

___To respond to conflict with others
"This is a way to deal with the conflict I have with someone. I couldn't cope with that individual (or group) very well otherwise."

___To rebel
"By doing this, I show others that I do what I want to do, not what others want me to do."

___To escape from the kids
"They could drive me crazy otherwise!"

D) Physical benefits

___To prevent or reduce physical pain
"It helps me cope with my pain (headaches, arthritis, injuries, surgical complications, chronic illness, or other physical pain)."

___To cope with craving
"It makes the craving go away."

___To give me energy to get things done
"I need it to do what I want (or need) to do."

___To enjoy sex more
"Sex just doesn't seem as good without it."

___To sleep better
"I can't get to sleep without it."

___To prevent physical withdrawal symptoms (this benefit mainly applies to substances, but in a psychological sense it might apply to any addiction) (NEW)
"If I don't keep using, I will have withdrawal symptoms."

E) Intellectual benefits

___To be more creative
"I don't think I can create what I want to and need to without doing this."

___To think better (or more clearly)
"I am aware of my thoughts better. They are clearer, not too fast and not too slow, and I can follow them more easily."

___To make painful memories go away
"I can't stand remembering those things, and when I do, it makes the memories go away."

F) Other benefits

___To test my self-control
"It gives me a chance to see how much I can handle."

___To have activity in my life
"If I don't do this, what else would I do?"

G) Benefits not mentioned

___To experience other benefits not yet mentioned. Although many specific benefits of addiction are listed above, it is impossible to list all of them, or to list each benefit in its varying degrees of intensity. List here any other benefits you experience currently with this addiction, and describe them as specifically as you can:

8. Review your checkmarks above. The items with three checkmarks are the primary benefits, for you, of this addiction, at this time. Make any revisions that now seem appropriate. For instance, an item that has two checkmarks may now seem like it merits one, or three checkmarks.

9. Do these benefits (all the items checked above) seem worthwhile to you? Do they seem like real and legitimate reasons to engage in your addiction? Can you identity any reasons why these benefits would not be valuable to you? (To repeat a point I made earlier, I am suggesting that the needs your addiction satisfies are fine in themselves, but the side effects of satisfying these needs with the addiction call into question whether to continue the addiction. It is not the needs that are the problem, but your method of satisfying them.)

10. Summarize in your own words the current benefits of your addiction:

11. How do the current benefits compare with the initial benefits (as identified in Chapter 3, Questions 6 through 9)?

12. If there are differences between current and initial benefits, what do you think these differences mean?

13. What immediate rewards could you establish for making progress in changing your addiction? Who would you like to be noticing the changes you make, and what would you like them to say?

Projects . . .

1. I suggested earlier that the benefits of an addiction tend to go away over time, but not entirely. I also suggested that even if the benefits have not yet diminished for you, they could eventually, and especially if your involvement in your addiction increases. Observe other individuals with your addiction who are more involved, or involved for longer than you are. How much benefit do they get from the addiction (regardless of the costs they experience)?

2. Identify changes that you could be making now, small steps in the direction of overcoming addiction, even if you are not ready for complete change. Establish a reward system for these small steps, and begin using it. What happens?

3. Identify someone close to you, and discuss changes you are focusing on in Project 2. Ask this individual to tell you when your successful behavior is noticed. Provide suggestions about what might be said to you, how it might be said, and when to say it. How hard is it to ask for this attention? How helpful is it to receive it?

What's Important Now?

If you date your answers to these questions, the answers over time will become a diary of your growth. It is likely that in future readings of this chapter different ideas will be important to you, reflecting the fact that you are indeed changing.

Which ideas from this chapter are most useful *to you, now*?

How can you put these ideas into action?

How much confidence do you have in your judgement in selecting these ideas as crucial at this time? (Circle a number; 10 is highest confidence)

0   1   2   3   4   5   6   7   8   9   10

5

The Current Costs of Addiction

> Socrates: *Did you not just say that virtue consists of desiring*
> *good things and experiences, and having*
> *the ability to get them?*
> Meno: *Yes, that is what I said.*
> Socrates: *And isn't the "desiring" part the same for*
> *everyone? Doesn't everyone desire what is good?*
> Meno: *Apparently.*
> Socrates: *Then if no one is better in desiring what is good,*
> *perhaps some are better at getting it?*
> Meno: *Yes.*
>
> -- Plato (c.428-348 BC), *Meno*, 78b
> Translated by A. T. Horvath

Overview

If a habit is excessively relied on as a coping method, it becomes an addiction. Although an addiction may still provide benefits, it also has costs. These costs may increase over time. Eventually they can greatly outweigh any current benefits of the involvement. Knowing and being able to recall the costs of involvement are essential to overcoming addiction.

Conducting a Cost-Benefit Analysis of Addiction

Ultimately, only you will be in a position to know the costs of your addiction, although trusted others may be helpful in reminding you about some of them. It is easy to forget what we might prefer not to remember!

These costs will have something in common with the costs others have experienced, either from the same addiction you have, or from other addictions. For that reason, reviewing the typical costs of addiction, listed at the end of this chapter, will likely be helpful to you. You may also have experienced unique costs from your addiction, depending on your circumstances. How serious these costs have been for you will depend on your circumstances. For instance, if you were a multi-millionaire, spending $2000 a month on cocaine might not be (relatively) expensive for you. However, $2000 a month may be more than you can afford!

The reason to change an addiction, ultimately, is that the costs have begun to outweigh the benefits. To make this suggestion clear, imagine a scenario I call the "perfect addiction." The perfect addiction is based on use of the "perfect substance."

This perfect substance:
⇒ is very inexpensive
⇒ is widely available
⇒ causes no medical or health problems
⇒ is entirely legal
⇒ is socially accepted by all elements of society
⇒ provides as good a chemically induced euphoria as can be imagined (but the euphoria can be turned off instantly at the user's wish)
⇒ causes no impairment of productivity or functioning
⇒ is accepted by all of your significant others
⇒ reduces bad feelings
⇒ enhances good feelings
⇒ has no adverse psychological effects
⇒ does not damage an unborn child
⇒ does not lead to any psychological or physical dependence
⇒ and in every other way one can imagine has absolutely no costs or negative consequences of any kind

If this substance were available, would you consider using it? Not only would you use it, we all would! As this imaginary scenario is set up, there are no negatives associated with the substance, and therefore there is no reason not to use it. There were also several good reasons to use it (euphoria, mood regulation).

Now, don't hold your breath; this substance is unlikely ever to be available, at least in our lifetimes. One psychopharmacologist suggested that, because intoxication seems to be a regular aspect of the human experience, we ought to commit ourselves to a national research project to discover a safe intoxicant. In a nation that wages a "war on drugs" funding for such a research project seems unlikely.

On the other hand, there are many relatively safe intoxicants available now. They are the usual ones, of course, and are safe in varying degrees, provided you do not overuse them. If you do overuse them, we call it addiction. The difference between safe intoxication and addiction is the weight of the negatives associated with the addiction. Take those negatives away (as in our imaginary example of the perfect substance), and the addiction disappears.

In this chapter we complete the cost-benefit analysis of your addiction (or addictions) that we began in Chapter 3. To show that the conclusion of this cost-benefit analysis is not necessarily always the same, let me propose two situations in which a cost-benefit analysis might suggest that involvement with a substance or activity would be better than non-involvement.

Imagine that someone dear to you is dying from cancer. There is no reasonable hope of a cure, and the pain is excruciating. The only painkiller that seems to work is morphine (which is related to heroin). The physician has limited the dose of morphine, even though in recent days a higher dose appears to be needed to combat the pain. The physician's explanation for the limited dose is that a higher dose might lead to a morphine addiction. Does it matter to you if your loved one develops a "morphine addiction"?

Before going further, let me clarify that physical dependence on a substance means that the user needs larger and larger doses of the substance to achieve the effect of the original (smaller) dose, and that withdrawal symptoms (possibly to include shaking, nausea, seizures, and in severe cases death) will occur if the substance is abruptly stopped. Although some individuals have both physical dependence (a physical process) on a substance along with addiction (a psychological process), these processes can operate independently. We could consider activity addictions as possibly involving a physical dependence on internally released substances (e.g., gambling might release adrenaline in the brain, and therefore gambling could be a physical dependence on adrenaline). But it is simpler, given the lack of definitive evidence for this view of gambling, to think of activity addictions as involving a psychological process but not a substance.

Back to the sad scenario of a loved one dying from cancer. Although with a sufficient painkilling dose a physical dependence on morphine might develop, is this morphine addiction? A cost-benefit analysis of the morphine use would suggest that physical dependence on morphine is a small price to pay in one's final days, if morphine eliminates pain.

Imagine that a smoker of several decades is dying of lung cancer. There is again little hope of a cure. The physician states that even at this late date giving up smoking may possibly improve longevity and some aspects of quality of life. What does a cost-benefit analysis of this individual's smoking reveal?

This example is more complex. I imagine that the cost-benefit analysis could go either way. I do not think that longevity or any of the physical aspects of quality of life will be the crucial elements in the analysis, however. It can be difficult to stop smoking. Is the effort worth a possible extra 10 minutes of life? Yes, the lungs might function a little better without the additional cigarettes, but what if smoking is one of this individual's few remaining pleasures? I suspect that the crucial issue will be how important it is for this individual to have a sense of victory over tobacco. I can imagine someone deciding to stop smoking, even at the end of life, "because I want to prove to myself that I can do it." On the other hand, many individuals in this situation might see no good reason to stop smoking with no long-term payoff possible.

With these two examples I hope to persuade you that a mindless conclusion that "my addiction is bad" is not what I am hoping to coax out of you. On the other hand, I hope that you are facing up to your addiction much sooner in life than the smoker above, and that there are many benefits still available to you if you overcome your addiction.

Remembering the costs of your addiction will be a crucial aspect of overcoming it. I suggested earlier (just before Question 1 in Chapter 3) that activating relevant memories was an important step in working on personal change issues. Activating relevant memories gets needed information onto your "work area" where the information can be used. During a craving positive memories of the addiction are highly activated. Unless craving is countered, negative addiction memories may not even occur. Unless countered, the cost-benefit analysis you conduct when you are craving is naturally slanted toward the benefits of the addiction. In Chapters 8, 9 and 10 we will discuss how to combat this situation. For now, in preparation for these three chapters, we are making a compelling list of costs of the addiction (if these costs in fact exist), so that you use them when you learn to counter craving.

Enabling

If you are reading this workbook with someone else's addiction in mind, probably the most important concept to consider for yourself is enabling. Enabling is shielding the addicted individual from the costs of addiction. This shielding changes the cost-benefit analysis by lowering the costs and thereby lowering motivation to change.

Ironically, enabling is typically a well-intentioned effort to be helpful to the addicted individual. These well intentioned efforts can take many forms, including making excuses for the individual to others, performing the individual's responsibilities, financially supporting the individual, staying around and accepting abuse or neglect so as not to let the individual be lonely, and similar activities.

In an ideal world partners and family and friends might immediately distance themselves from addictive behavior. However, many times the addicted individual is still relied on, and distancing is not easy. A classic example is the woman with children who has not been previously employed outside the home, and who relies for financial support solely on her addicted and abusive but still employed husband. In this case shielding him from the consequences of his actions (like getting fired) is also shielding herself. We can understand why she might call the boss to say his Monday morning hangover is a cold!

If you are involved with an addicted individual, become as independent of the individual as you can, develop new support systems for yourself, and to the extent feasible let the costs of addiction fall on the individual not yourself. If distancing yourself (or even departing) from the relationship becomes desirable and feasible, recognize that this cost may or may not be motivating to the individual. Decide to distance yourself or not by what it will do for you, not what it might do for the individual.

Addiction and the Disadvantaged

One way to describe what motivates someone to overcome an addiction is that the individual realizes that there is "something to lose" by continuing the addiction. Although addicted individuals lose many things that others think should be valuable to them, they are in my experience quite careful about what is truly important to them. Sometimes they miscalculate, of course, and over time what is important to someone can also change under the influence of addictive experience. However, if there is little to lose (as in the case of the terminal cancer patient), addiction is in little conflict with anything else and therefore may continue.

Another case where someone may have or seem to have little to lose is someone in poverty, especially if this poverty is compounded by lack of education, lack of a supportive social network and no clear prospects for progress. Add addiction to this picture. What are the chances this individual will be motivated to overcome addiction?

In varying degrees the above scenario exists across this country (and the world). For many of these individuals the primary reason not to be *more* involved in addiction is that they can't afford to. On the other hand, being a drug dealer may provide access to money and more substances or other addictive experiences. Given where the individual started from, it is easy to see that there might be some confusion about whether being a drug dealer is a step forward or a step backward.

I do not know how these observations could translate into public policy and public health decisions. I do believe that any effort to fight a "war on drugs" that is not about helping addicted individuals to develop "something to lose" (other than losing freedom by going to prison) is not going to work well. Perhaps having a police state (which is about what we do have in many inner cities) is, after all, the simplest way to handle this problem. On the other hand, it may be possible to build up the lives of all of us, not just those who are in the stock market. I am not suggesting that we are morally obligated to do this, that we could afford to do it, or that it is even possible to do it. I do wonder what it will cost if we don't do it. I think we at least ought to talk about it.

Questions . . .

We begin this set of Questions by activating significant memories about your addiction, focusing on the costs of addiction in the current time period. Let "current" be whatever time period you used to answer the questions in Chapter 4. Because of this focus on costs, you are unlikely to experience a craving. However, if you do, just focus on this workbook, and the craving will go away.

1. Recall a recent *typical* experience with this addiction. Describe what happened. Focus on what seemed uncomfortable, painful, negative, costly, bad or dangerous about this experience.

2. Recall a recent *highly negative* experience with this addiction. By "highly negative" experience I especially mean one that got you thinking that it might be time to make changes in your addiction. Perhaps you can even recall the specific experience that persuaded you to read this workbook. Describe what happened. Focus on what seemed uncomfortable, painful, negative, costly, bad or dangerous about this experience.

3. Recall another recent highly negative experience with this addiction. Describe what happened. Focus on what seemed uncomfortable, painful, negative, costly, bad or dangerous about this experience.

4. If recalling additional negative experiences seems potentially helpful, describe these as well.

5. The experiences described above can help you answer the critical question of this chapter: What does this addiction now cost you? The checklist below will help you make sure that you have considered the full range of costs, problems and negatives possible from your addictive experience.

The categories of costs are not important and are placed here only because they might help you to identify commonalities across your costs. What is most important is not to miss any costs. Ignore the categories if they are distracting.

It may be tempting to minimize the costs of your addiction. Regardless of how you describe the costs, however, you are still experiencing them. Your experience will not modify itself to fit your description of it. Those who ignore history are condemned to repeat it. Those who ignore reality are still affected by it. Better to be honest and accurate now, to prevent the possibility of worse problems in the future. As a check on yourself, you might get a trusted other to review your answers. As we did in Project 2 in Chapter 2, this review could actually take place, or happen only in imagination.

On the list below check off each item that applies to your *current* involvement with this addiction. Place three checkmarks if the cost strongly applies, one checkmark if the cost is noticeable but not very strong or regular, and two checkmarks if it is in between. Then, in the space below each checked item, write a brief reminder to yourself of one or more examples of experiencing that cost.

My addiction leads to:

A) Emotional costs

___fear and anxiety
(feelings like anxiety, tension, fear, stress, agitation, nervousness, vulnerability, intimidation, embarrassment or panic; may be accompanied by withdrawal from feared situations)

___sadness and depression
(feelings like depression, sadness, hurt, discouragement, grief, feeling defeated, feeling deprived or feeling abandoned)

___anger
(feelings like frustration, resentment, anger, annoyance, irritability or rage; may be accompanied by aggressive behavior)

___shame or guilt
(feelings like remorse, being ashamed, or feeling guilty or responsible. I am really upset about what I have done)

___disgust or distaste
(being disgusted by what I have done)

___boredom
(feeling bored, apathetic, or impatient)

___overexcitement
(being too excited, being too sexual, being too impulsive)

___emotional exhaustion
(nothing left inside of me)

___a sense of separateness or aloneness
(feeling unable to connect with anyone or anything)

___emotional instability
(feelings change rapidly and excessively, and seem out of control)

___feeling generally bad, negative, pessimistic or in pain
(the possibility of pleasure or happiness may seem to have diminished or disappeared)

___feeling worthless
(having little or no confidence, or little sense of being valuable)

___feeling dead
(going through the motions of living, but not really feeling alive)

___feeling suicidal

___feeling crazy, abnormal, or strange
(or that my life is this way)

___feeling out of control
(feeling as if I am not in charge of my life anymore, the addiction is)

___other negative feelings
(loneliness, envy, suspiciousness, alienation, humiliation, shock, feeling
powerless or other negative feelings)

___I have been diagnosed with behavioral/emotional disorders that definitely or
probably arose from or were made worse by my addiction.

B) Social costs

___not fitting in well anymore
(with family, friends, usual acquaintances or groups)

___decreased social ability
(no longer interested or able to connect with others)

___conflict with others
(they object to changes in me)

___spending time with others whom I don't really respect or like

___having less time to spend with individuals I care about

___disruption or ending of the central relationships in my life
(loss of trust or respect, arguments, hostility)

C) *Physical and health costs*

___poorer general health
(poor nutrition, weight gain or loss, low energy)

___infections or disorders caused by the addiction
(HIV, hepatitis, cirrhosis, cancer, nasal problems, cough, injuries from accidents, heart attack, high blood pressure, menstrual dysfunction, seizures, internal bleeding, stroke,)

___poor personal hygiene and unhealthy appearance
(yellow teeth, track marks, poor complexion, bad breath, dental problems)

___physical pains and dysfunctions
(hangovers, headaches, vomiting, diarrhea)

___repeated craving

___lowered energy and endurance

___less enjoyment of sex
(sexual dysfunction)

___poor sleep
(trouble falling asleep, trouble staying asleep, nightmares, restlessness)

___psychotic symptoms
(auditory, visual or tactile hallucinations; delusions)

___withdrawal symptoms
(this cost mainly applies to some substances, but in a psychological sense it might apply to any addiction)

___impairment of the health of my unborn child
(this cost is usually thought to apply mainly or only to women, but so much is unknown about the effects of addiction that men would do well to consider this cost for themselves also)

D) Intellectual costs

___lowered creativity

___less ability to think clearly

___poorer memory

E) Work and productivity costs

___less ability to work, learn, or be productive

___excessive time missed from work or school

___impaired ability to drive or operate machinery

___accidents caused or contributed to by the addiction

___being less productive or capable on hobbies or personal interests

___having less time for activities of interest to me

F) *Financial costs*

___less money
(estimate how much money the addiction has cost, using the following categories and adding other categories if relevant):

      money spent directly on the addiction

      money spent on coping with the consequences of the addiction

      money spent on interest (for loans arising from the addiction)

      money lost because less was earned

      money lost because opportunities were not acted on

      savings spent

___debts brought on by the addiction

___taxes unpaid

___stress associated with financial problems

___difficulty paying for basic obligations and needs

G) *Time lost*

___time lost to the addiction
(estimate how much time the addiction has cost, using the following categories and adding other categories if relevant):

      time spent directly on the addiction (including preparing to engage in it, engaging in it, and recovering from engaging in it)

      time spent on coping with the consequences of the addiction

time wasted avoiding important activities, because I felt unable to face them

H) Legal costs

___DUI, other arrests, convictions, fines, legal obligations, jail or prison time, probation, parole

I) Reductions in personal integrity

___being dishonest with others

___being dishonest with myself

___feeling little or no self-respect

___being irresponsible about important obligations

___letting down people I care about

___acting in conflict with my deeper values

___acting in conflict with my spiritual self (or in conflict with God)

J) Costs not mentioned

___other costs not yet mentioned. Although many specific costs of addiction are listed above, it is impossible to list all of them, or to list each cost in its varying degrees of severity. List here any other costs you experience currently with this addiction, and describe them as specifically as you can:

6. Review your checkmarks above. The items with three checkmarks are the primary costs, for you, of this addiction, at this time. Make any revisions that now seem appropriate. For instance, an item that has two checkmarks may now seem like it merits one, or three checkmarks.

7. Do these costs (all the items checked above) seem significant to you? Do they seem like real and legitimate reasons to overcome the addiction? Can you identity any reasons why these costs would not be significant to you?

8. Notice that you have probably not checked all of the costs above, and indeed, may have checked only a few of them. Do you feel fortunate? How pleased are you that you are facing up to this addiction before even more problems develop? If you continue with the addiction, which costs are likely to show up next? Which current costs are likely to get significantly worse? If you had overcome the addiction at the first sign of trouble, what costs might you have prevented?

9. Summarize in your own words the current costs of your addiction:

10. In Chapter 4 I suggested that one of the ironies of addiction is that over time it tends to take away from you what it gave you at first. Notice that the checklist above parallels the checklists in Chapters 3 and 4. Compare the current costs of addiction, with the initial benefits (as identified in Chapter 3, Questions 6 through 9). To what extent has addiction taken away from you what it first gave you?

11. You are about to complete the cost-benefit analysis. The current costs (above) and the current benefits (in Chapter 4, Questions 6 through 10) have been identified. Review them again if there is a chance that your thinking about them has changed. For instance, a change in your answers to Questions in Chapters 3 and 4 might have occurred as a result of reflections you made when answering the Questions in Chapter 5.

Compare the costs and the benefits, for you at this time, for this addiction. What conclusions do you reach?

12. If you are having difficulty reaching a conclusion, you may want to consider making a transformation in how you are looking at the costs and benefits. Instead of evaluating costs of the addiction vs. benefits of the addiction, you might transform "costs of the addiction" into "benefits of overcoming the addiction." Then you would compare the benefits of the addiction vs. the benefits of overcoming it. If above you checked having less money as a cost of the addiction, just reverse this cost to get a benefit of overcoming the addiction, which in this case would be having more money. Does this way of looking at the comparison make it easier? What conclusions do you reach?

13. You may have reached a firm conclusion about your cost-benefit analysis, and a firm decision as well: "I need to overcome this addiction!" If so, the remainder of this workbook will help you follow through on this decision. State your decision in your own words:

Perhaps you have reached the conclusion that the costs of your involvement do not outweigh the benefits, and therefore you are going to continue your involvement with that substance or activity. As we have already stated, if the costs don't outweigh the benefits, then you have a habit not an addiction. I caution you to remember the warning above (about being honest with yourself), to consider discussing your conclusion with a trusted other, and to reevaluate your conclusion at some reasonable point in the future. Lastly, if the costs are significant, even if they are outweighed by the benefits, it may still be worth changing your involvement. In particular the next chapter on alternative coping methods may be relevant.

On the other hand, you may still be hesitating to reach a decision to overcome the addiction, even if the cost-benefit analysis suggests the wisdom of this decision. If any of the following reasons seem applicable to you, write more detail on your thinking:

I am concerned that the benefits of overcoming the addiction may be a long way off, or not ever attainable by me, so why bother?

I don't think I will be able to make the change

It doesn't seem like the right time to make a change

I want to make some minor adjustments in the addiction first, to see how much they help, before jumping into any big commitment to change

(In the next chapter we will discuss ways to identify and correct any irrational thoughts in the answers to Question 13)

Projects . . .

1. One of the best ways to bring about a personal change is to imagine that the change has already occurred, and then act accordingly. If you want to feel self-confident, imagine that you already are self-confident, then just act that way. In time your feeling of self-confidence will catch up with your behavior. Of course, a little coaching on how to act self-confident might be helpful. But it is amazing how one can act a certain way, if you have some idea of what to do, even if the feelings aren't there yet.

It's time to act like you don't have the addiction, to try this way of being on for size. Pick a suitable time period, perhaps a few hours or a day or two, and select a few benefits of overcoming the addiction to keep in mind. For instance, suppose that your addiction costs include feeling guilty, not spending enough time with loved ones, and not being fully productive at work. Pick a time when, to the extent you can, you will act responsibly, spend time with loved ones, and work hard. How do you like the experience? Would it be good to have it all the time?

What's Important Now?

(If you date your answers to these questions, the answers over time will become a diary of your growth. It is likely that in future readings of this chapter different ideas will be important to you, reflecting the fact that you are indeed changing.

Which ideas from this chapter are most useful *to you, now*?

How can you put these ideas into action?

How much confidence do you have in your judgement in selecting these ideas as crucial at this time? (Circle a number; 10 is highest confidence)

0   1   2   3   4   5   6   7   8   9   10

Coping And Connecting

Overview

There are many ways to cope with any need or problem. You have identified the needs that your addiction satisfies. You could learn new coping methods, ones which would not cost as much as the addiction. There are many options for learning new coping methods. Almost all of these options involve learning from or learning with others. Learning and overcoming isolation are related projects. We need to balance learning independently with being tutored, and being independent with connecting with others.

Any Problem Has Multiple Solutions

Suppose that you use your addiction to cope with loneliness and anxiety. Do you think that this is the only way to do it? Don't other individuals, who do not use addiction, find other ways to cope with loneliness and anxiety?

For instance, if you are lonely, you can work on learning how to be a better friend and learning how to meet others so that you can get to know them. As you know more about being a friend and meeting others, you can keep looking for potential friends. You can also select a variety of places and activities at which to meet individuals with different interests. Eventually you will have more friends in your life. Additionally, you could learn to cope better with times when you are alone by developing more hobbies and activities, and engaging in them regularly. You might develop some relationships with individuals at a distance, with whom you could communicate by phone or letter or e-mail. You might rebuild established relationships that have been less active. You might throw yourself into working for a cause that you are passionate about, and there meet others with the same passion. You might develop a reading plan (for instance, to study a particular period in history), and get to know through their work the different authors who write about that historical period. Any of these solutions is likely to be much less costly than continuing an addiction.

Learn From Others

Most of what we learn comes from others. This information comes either through direct interaction, or indirect interaction, when we read their writings or otherwise observe what they have left for us to consider. Do you remember as a child or young adult seeking out information about something that was very important to you? Do you remember how carefully you questioned others, or read new information? Do you remember how you sought out different perspectives from different individuals, to make sure you were not unduly influenced by just one individual or author? Everyone has had a version of these experiences, because everyone is curious about something. To paraphrase Aristotle, the 4th century BC Greek philosopher, all individuals by nature desire to learn. I'll add that the easiest way to learn is to be taught by someone who already knows. Of course, many behaviors still need to be practiced, but here as well the practice will be more effective if it is guided by accurate knowledge from someone who can already do the behavior or has experience teaching it.

There is a distinction between being able to teach something, and being able to do it. We expect that a good coach will be able to do, at some level, what is being taught, but we don't expect the coach to be the best at it. The best swimming coach is not necessarily the best swimmer. In order to be most efficient as a learner, we probably would do well to have both models of excellent performance to observe and skilled teachers to guide us.

It is rare for any of us to be the first one to know or be able to do something substantially different. Even these new behaviors and knowledge are not entirely new, but also contain components of established behavior and knowledge. Of course, we may organize our knowledge and behavior according to our own style and ideas, and there may be significant creativity to this. But even here, we can probably trace the influences of others. I am not elaborating this point to make you feel incompetent. Rather, I hope you will recognize that because most of what you know has come from interacting with others, the way to proceed now is to seek others out, not isolate yourself. What you need know is already known by someone else, probably many people. Find them!

Be Involved With Others

There is a second equally important reason to seek out others. In relationships with others we can experience and understand ourselves, accept ourselves, and overcome aloneness (possibly the greatest human problem). Aristotle also wrote, again to paraphrase, that human beings are social beings. Human happiness comes not only from gaining mastery, as we have been discussing in these last few paragraphs, but also from being in relationship with others. Freud said it perhaps most simply: the mature person can both love and work.

Just as there are many different types of learning interactions, there are many different types of relationships. It is desirable to be connected to many others in many different ways. It is probable that individuals with a breadth of quality relationships are unlikely to develop significant addiction or other behavioral problems. This does not mean that we need to have ten best friends and hundreds of acquaintances. It is possible to have only a few very close relationships, but the quality of these and the diversity of our other relationships are as strong a shield against emotional and behavioral problems as one can have.

Consider this perspective in terms of the cost-benefit analysis of addiction, just completed in Chapters 3 to 5. If you had been more closely involved with others, might the costs of addiction have become apparent more quickly (because several caring others might have discussed them with you sooner)? Would less isolation make or have made overcoming addiction easier? Assuming you have at least a few close relationships, their level of closeness and openness, and level of commitment are the primary factors. Breadth of relationships is a second factor. We need a diversity of people to interact with. We experience different parts of ourselves as we interact with different people in different ways. We have a much broader concept of ourselves as we have breadth of social interaction. That broader concept gives us a greater variety of perspectives to use when solving problems.

Consider the settings discussed in the next several pages. How might you use them for interacting with others? They are relevant to learning new coping skills, overcoming addiction, learning anything else, and being connected to others (even if only indirectly in some cases). For each setting I mention some aspects of its opportunities for learning or connecting, especially those relevant to this workbook. I hope the list will stimulate you to consider the settings you already frequent, and settings you might explore.

◆ **Reading**. Although we are to some extent at the mercy of circumstance when it comes to meeting interesting, compatible and helpful companions, most of us have great access to authors. Most librarians are delighted to track down books for the truly interested reader. Although the dialogue with an author is one-sided, the process of understanding an author is a kind of conversation. Many dedicated readers feel themselves to be in relationships with selected authors. In my early years of specializing in alternative addiction treatment, when I would get discouraged about the slowness with which the field was changing, I would occasionally return to one of the books on addiction I particularly admired. I felt comfort just reading it, and while I was doing so, I no longer felt so alone.

With respect to learning self-help skills specifically, there are many excellent self-help books. Those that have a cognitive-behavioral therapy (CBT) orientation will be consistent with the orientation of this workbook. Here are several ways to identify these books:

1. If you want to be comprehensive, consult *The Authoritative Guide to Self-Help Books,* by Santrock, Minnett, and Campbell, published by Guilford Publications (1994). Approximately 350 self-help books in 33 categories are rated, based on a survey of 500 behavioral health professionals. I consult this book frequently.

2. Consult catalogs of publishers and distributors who specialize in self-help books. They may also carry other media and professional materials. Most will send a catalog for free. Some prominent ones include:

    The Albert Ellis Institute, 800-323-IRET
    Impact Publishers, 800-2-IMPACT, www.impactpublishers.com
    New Harbinger Publications, 800-748-6273
    The Psychological Corporation, 800-228-0752
    Research Press, 800-519-2707, www.researchpress.com

3. Self-help books I often recommend include:

    Anger: The Misunderstood Emotion, by Carol Tavris
    Your Perfect Right, by Robert Alberti and Michael Emmons (assertiveness)
    Feeling Good, by David Burns (overcoming depression)
    The Feeling Good Handbook, by David Burns (overcoming depression)
    Mind over Mood, by Greenberger and Padesky (overcoming depression)
    Learned Optimism, by Martin Seligman
    Beyond the Relaxation Response, by Herbert Bensen (stress management)
    Self-Esteem, by Matt McKay and Partick Fanning
    Messages, by Matt McKay, Margaret Davis and Patrick Fanning (communication)
    What Color is Your Parachute?, by Richard Bolles (choosing a career)
    SOS! Help for Parents, by Lynn Clark (parenting)
    Parenting the Strong-willed Child, by Rex Forehand and Nicholas Long
    Love is Never Enough, by Aaron Beck (couples)

4. For books and other media that cover both alternative coping methods and overcoming addiction, consult "Bibliography and Resources," and the SMART Recovery Recommended Reading List in the back of this workbook.

◆ **Audiotapes or radio.** In addition to the above distributors, there are companies that specialize in providing audiotapes of book recordings or lectures. If you do much driving, or have visual difficulties, audiotapes are a great option.
   Audio Editions, 800-231-4261
   Books on Tape, 800-626-3333
   The Teaching Company, 800-203-7799 (videos also)

Radio programming is not usually printed in advance. However, you may find a helpful talk show. You may even want to call in! Consistent with the above observation that some individuals perceive themselves to be in relationship with authors, even more so in contemporary society can we develop a form of relationship with individuals we "interact" with only by listening to them on radio, or watching them on television or in movies. As long as these relationships are only a portion of the relationships we have, they contribute to relationship breadth.

◆ **Videotapes or television.** The book distributors that carry audiotapes often carry videotapes. Also investigate public television and other educationally oriented channels.

◆ **Plays or movies.** Many movies address fundamental human conflicts and ways to deal with them. Plays do so even more because compared to movies sets are minimal and the focus is on the actors and their dialogue. You may be able to identify plays and movies in which characters face problems similar to your own. I also recommend seeing some comedies! If you prefer reading, try novels.

◆ **Lectures** (talks, presentations, speeches). A local publication may carry a listing of local lectures. Colleges and universities often bring in speakers on fascinating subjects. A local mental health center may be able to tell you about local lectures on behavioral health topics. Often they are free. Lectures can be primarily learning opportunities (listening to the lecturer), and also social opportunities (meeting the other listeners).

◆ **Classes.** In addition to formal educational institutions, a variety of other organizations offer ongoing or one-time classes or workshops. Like lectures, classes are both learning and social opportunities. Many organizations offer classes on behavioral health topics.

◆ **Support or discussion groups.** Despite the American emphasis on support group attendance, I want to emphasize that these groups are not essential for overcoming addiction. Social support for overcoming addiction is critical, but that support does not necessarily need to be obtained in an addiction support group. They can be helpful, however, and are especially a good option for someone whose immediate social environment is not broad enough.

1. *Alternative support groups.* Over the last two decades several alternative support groups for addiction have emerged. *SMART Recovery*, an abstinence group for any type of addiction, and *Moderation Management* (MM), a moderation or abstinence group for drinking, have approaches consistent with the approach of this workbook. The others groups fall somewhere in the middle of a "scientific perspective" continuum that has SMART and MM at one end and 12-step groups at the other.

The main problem with these alternatives is that they are not widely available. According to AA's 1996 Membership survey it has over 96,000 weekly meetings worldwide (most are in the U.S.). SMART has about 250, and MM about 50, almost all of which are in the U.S. For those with e-mail both SMART and MM have Internet listserve discussion groups.

Individual alternative group meetings are dependent on the ability of the leader (usually a volunteer peer) to lead a helpful group. The meeting leaders of the alternatives are comparable to "sponsors" in the 12-step groups. Sponsors meet individually with 12-step members to support their progress. Some sponsors and meeting leaders are better than others. Having a good sponsor may be essential to working the 12 steps well. Having a good alternative meeting leader may be essential to having a good meeting. Many of the sponsors and leaders are excellent.

All of the alternative groups have a discussion format (as opposed to the sequential monologue format of a regular AA meeting). Participants engage in discussion with one another, rather than listening to a series of unconnected monologues. AA also has speaker meetings, which are essentially lectures, as well as other types of meetings. The discussion format is probably better than the monologue format for providing social support for participants. If a leader oversteps his or her role, the group is available as a buffer to prevent significant abuse. The private meetings between sponsor and sponsee are highly conducive to experiencing social support, but there is also a risk that the sponsor can have a negative effect, particularly if the sponsor oversteps his or her role and becomes domineering. The alternative support groups do not have sponsors.

Alternative Support Groups

Self Management And Recovery Training
SMART Recovery (SMART)
24000 Mercantile Road, Suite 11
Beachwood, Ohio 44122
216-292-0220
FAX 831-3776
SRMail1@aol.com
www.smartrecovery.org
To subscribe to SMARTREC, post listserv@maelstrom.stjohns.edu with the following message:
subscribe SMARTREC yourfirstname yourlastname

Moderation Management (MM)
P.O. Box 1752
Woodinville, WA 98072
425-844-8228
www.moderation.org
To subscribe to MM, post listserv@maelstrom.stjohns.edu with the following message:
subscribe MM yourfirstname yourlastname

Women for Sobriety (WFS)
P.O. Box 618
Quakertown, PA 18951-0618
215-536-8026 (voice and fax)
WFSobriety@aol.com
www.mediapulse.com/wfs/

Men for Sobriety (MFS)
(same as Women for Sobriety)

Rational Recovery Systems (RR)
Box 800
Lotus, CA 95651
916-621-4374
916-621-2667 (voice and fax)
800-303-CURE
rr@rational.org
www.rational.org/recovery

Secular Organizations for Sobriety/Save Our Selves (SOS)
5521 Grosvenor Blvd.
Los Angeles, CA 90066
310-821-8430
FAX 821-2610
(unofficial website) www.unhooked.com

2. *12-step groups*. As previously mentioned, I recommend attending a 12-step meeting if you have never attended one. If alternative support groups are not available to you, attending 12-step groups might be considered, as described in Chapter 2. Alcoholics Anonymous is listed in every American phonebook. AA may be able to direct you to other groups, if they are not also listed (Cocaine Anonymous, Narcotics Anonymous, Pills Anonymous, Overeaters Anonymous, etc.).

There is probably no other single place one could find such a wealth of recovering models. There is a good likelihood of your finding someone reasonably similar to yourself. Finding a good model is discussed below. If you are able to look past your disagreements with the 12-step philosophy, and not feel pressured by being an "outsider," 12-step meetings might have something to offer you.

Although there are aspects of the 12-step approach that are inaccurate from a scientific perspective (and many that are not), I believe that spiritual considerations make this fact irrelevant for individuals committed to 12-step recovery. This is appropriate, in that the scientific and spiritual realms are separate. I believe that what happens in one is ultimately irrelevant to the other. Science will never prove or disprove the existence of any God or higher power. Spiritual success, however one defines it, will not come from scientific knowledge.

If everyone who needed recovery could accept the 12-step spiritual approach (there are also alternative spiritual approaches), then this workbook would be unneeded. However, if you want to pursue overcoming addiction from a practical perspective (many do and this does not mean they are unspiritual), alternatives are needed.

3. *Local clearinghouses*. Check for a local clearinghouse that lists local support groups for problems other than addiction. Listed here is contact information for the American Self-help Clearinghouse, which has information on nationally and regionally available support groups (including addiction, emotional problems, health problems, etc.).

American Self-Help Clearinghouse
Northwest Covenant Medical Center
25 Pocono Road
Denville, NJ 07834
Group Information: 973-625-7101
TDD: 973-625-9053
FAX: 973-625-8848
Administration: 973-625-9565

4. *Informal groups* on almost any topic are constantly springing up. Years ago there were "users groups" for individuals who used a particular brand of computer or software or hardware. (These groups seem to have been replaced by Internet interactions.) If there is a topic you are interested in, there probably is a group somewhere talking about it. Because the Internet transcends geographical limitations, it may be one of the best places to look for what you want, but it is not the only place.

◆ **Professionally led educational groups**. You can discover these meetings as you also investigate local behavioral health lectures and local support groups. These groups are similar to support groups, except that having a professional leader increases the likelihood of a well-run meeting. The leader is probably also a specialist in the topic area and may have valuable information and insights to present.

◆ **Group psychotherapy**. Group psychotherapy is intended for individuals who are willing to attend a group consistently and participate actively in the discussion. You can "hide" in a support group or educational group. If a group has a specific content focus (e.g., relapse prevention, surviving a breakup, assertiveness training), it may be similar to the professionally led educational group. The more unscripted type, process group psychotherapy, focuses on the concerns that the participants bring to the group (their own emotional and behavioral "issues"). It also focuses on the "group process," which is the participants' collective and individual behavior in the group. In many ways process group psychotherapy is the most demanding and potentially most helpful psychotherapeutic experience. In any psychotherapy the client can report on outside problems. In individual therapy sometimes problems are evidenced by client behavior in the session. This in-the-session demonstration of problems is much more likely in a group, where there are perhaps 6 to 10 other individuals to be reacting to.

◆ **Individual coaching or instruction**. This might also be called tutoring or education, done one-on-one, as opposed to the group format of a class. A variety of professionals, teachers, coaches, mentors, or counselors might provide it. For specialized skills and knowledge, particularly for someone who wants to become an expert in a particular area, this is probably the educational setting of choice. Moving to Florida so your child can attend a year round tennis camp, in hopes of turning pro, would be an example of this. Classes are less expensive versions of this interaction.

◆ **Individual or couples psychotherapy or counseling**. Individual therapy is the setting of choice if you have much talking you want to do, want complete confidentiality, and want a listener who is also an expert on behavioral and emotional issues. Couples sessions offer the same benefits. Licensed professionals include psychologists and social workers. Psychiatrists can also do this, but they tend to emphasize medication and de-emphasize talking. Psychiatric medication is invaluable for some individuals (see Chapter 8). If you are seeing a psychiatrist (or other physician) for medication, you may also want to see a psychotherapist. Some states may also license additional types of counselors.

Individual therapy is also the setting of choice for developing new coping methods if you have significant levels of depression, anxiety, or anger, or if you have any other significant emotional or behavioral problems. Major relationship problems also may not improve without professional help. A psychotherapist can guide you to books, local and other resources, and save you much time in finding appropriate ones. Because of a psychotherapist's training, there may be no one who understands your unique situation as well, or who can suggest as many useful options and alternatives for you to consider.

I believe that either individual psychotherapy or couples therapy (as noted below) are also the settings of choice for treating addiction (for those who need treatment). Unlike traditional treatment, which is mostly conducted in educational groups such that every client covers every topic, individual treatment is flexible. The range of problems a group of addiction clients brings to treatment can be enormous. A pre-established group curriculum is unlikely to cover them adequately. Individual or couples sessions, supplemented by selected educational groups and group therapy, could cover a basic curriculum (such as the one provided in this workbook) and add anything else needed.

The quality of the help you receive will depend on many factors, including the knowledge and skill of the professional you consult, the working relationship you develop, the effort you put in between sessions, and your willingness to be open about what you really think and feel. The therapist is not a magician or a mind reader. If you don't exert effort, the therapist cannot make change happen magically. If you don't tell the therapist what is really going on, a good one will know something important is missing, but probably won't know exactly what it is. How can a therapist help solve a problem that you don't talk about?

◆ **Discussion with trusted others**. There is a wide range of others you may trust to converse with, including partners, immediate family, extended family, friends, and clergy. There are also a number of ways to communicate, including face to face, phone, mail, e-mail, and others. A crucial issue here, as with therapy, is the extent to which your listener is helping you to arrive at your own solutions instead of imposing solutions from outside.

This is not to say we don't benefit from occasional advice and information. But your listener's primary perspective needs to be helping you understand yourself, not helping you understand the listener (who has now turned into a talker!). The factors that are important in psychotherapy are also important in this similar type of relationship.

Until this point I have been implying that learning new coping methods is primarily about gathering new information or self-understanding. However, for many of us the behaviors and responses that we need to cope are already there; we just don't use them enough or at the right time. To take an assertiveness example, everyone can say "no," but saying it firmly, to the right person, at the right time is another matter. It is in our ongoing relationships that another major factor in learning mostly operates, the factor of *reinforcement and punishment*.

Despite the seriousness of some conversations with those close to us, most of our interactions with them are casual and often contain a substantial nonverbal component. For instance, you learn that you did well at something, and that your partner is pleased, by a facial expression or tone of voice. Although interactions with others are well suited to gathering information, interactions with those close to us are also well suited to providing reinforcement and punishment for specific behavior. This reinforcement and punishment is often crucial in supporting or detracting from any effort at change.

Ideally, those around you will provide meaningful reinforcements of your changes and avoid punishments that are counterproductive. Because even those who know you well may not realize how you will react as you attempt new behaviors, you might want to suggest to them what you would find helpful and not helpful. If they are willing to accept it, be specific about words to use and accompanying nonverbal behavior. For instance, you could tell your partner "when I get upset like that, I would prefer that you not say anything for a few minutes, until I speak first; once I have started talking, it will mean I am calm enough to discuss it; while you are waiting, I would prefer that you not look at me, because that will just make it harder for me to calm down; in time I hope to be able not to get so upset to start with; would all that be OK with you?"

In Chapter 1 I described addiction as a psychological problem. There are some individuals about whom we might say that it is equally a social problem. I will discuss in Chapter 7 how we control ourselves by controlling the situations we are in. Most of the time the crucial aspects of situations are interpersonal. If you are having difficulty overcoming addiction, your interpersonal environment and your reactions to it are good places to consider making additional changes.

Although this workbook has focused primarily on you as an individual, the ideas you learn from it may not be enough for you to overcome addiction if there are too many difficulties in your immediate interpersonal environment. I do not mean to suggest that there is something wrong with the others around you, or with you. However, communication and reinforcement patterns can become established and rigidly fixed to the extent that professional counseling is indicated to change them. Love is the best drug, but as Sartre observed, hell is other people. As progress is made on changing communication and reinforcement patterns, progress on overcoming addiction becomes more likely. There is a saying that you should avoid doctors unless you are really sick. I suggest that this saying applies here. Although you could wait for a change of circumstances to possibly change the negative interactional patterns, you would be trusting to fate if you don't take matters into your own hands by seeking treatment.

On the other hand, you know your close relationships are going well when most of the time:
⇒ conflict and feelings are discussed openly (without blaming or ridiculing)
⇒ you carefully listen to each other
⇒ there are few secrets
⇒ mistakes are admitted
⇒ compromises are made
⇒ you enjoy being with each other
⇒ you pay attention to each other in a positive way
⇒ you know you can rely on one another
⇒ you give and receive in about equal amounts

◆ **Discussion with acquaintances** (neighbors, coworkers, colleagues, members of groups we belong to, etc.). These relationships are less intense than our close relationships, but having a breadth of them, as suggested earlier, gives us an opportunity to experience different aspects of ourselves. Others are like mirrors; they reflect back to us different parts of ourselves. The more mirrors we look into, the more parts we see. Having a diversity of "parts" is an advantage in solving problems, when it is desirable to have the capacity to flexibly consider a problem from different perspectives.

◆ **Observing any good model**. The main issues here are finding a good model and getting into a good position to observe the model. This is easier to accomplish with physical skills than emotional ones. However, if there is someone you know who is good at something you want to learn, keep an eye on this individual!

Another factor in choosing a model, if you are able to control it, is to find someone who is somewhat better than you are, but not overwhelmingly better. When there is a great distance between ourselves and the model, or the model is dramatically different from us in other ways, the model's actions are less relevant to us. Watching Michael Jordan's driving slam dunk may be inspiring, but not too pertinent if you are just learning how to dribble!

At the other end of the spectrum, much learning from others is quite casual and not deliberately sought out. I might observe how someone wears certain clothes, handles a compliment, eats a certain food, deals with teenagers, or organizes a hard disk drive. If you are mindful, you may discover many useful pieces of information, even ones you did not seek. To put it another way, the individuals you spend time around may have a bigger influence on you than you realize.

◆ **Doing any of the above in imagination**. One fascinating aspect of our brains is how some information can most easily be retrieved using imagination. As mentioned in Chapter 2, it is possible to have an imaginary conversation with someone, and have that person "say" something in the imaginary conversation. We might not have been able to predict well what this person would "say." The way to get at the information is to have the "conversation." If there is someone whose input you would like, and the person is not otherwise available to you, your imagination may be the way to get it. Imagination is a strong factor in the one-sided relationships we have with authors and media personalities.

◆ **Other options**. Combinations of the above interactions also occur. Traditional addiction treatment is typically a combination of classes, educational groups, support groups, individual coaching (with a 12-step sponsor), and possibly group therapy or individual therapy.

Balancing Learning and Connections to Others

As you consider the above interactions, I hope you see the potential for learning, as well as the potential for social support. Having social support includes the sense of being connected to others who care about what happens to you. As much as any helpful information you will learn, the caring of others is crucial to most changes you will make. Love is the best drug. Therefore, even if you think you know everything about some change you are making, make sure in addition that you have the social support, through one or more of the above interactions, to help you follow through.

You may know of some perspectives that encourage a "rugged individualism" approach to life. I suggest a balance between going one's own way and being connected to others. You may recall the distinction between warm- and cold-blooded animals. The distinction is often presented as follows: The cold-blooded animal takes on the temperature of its surroundings and may not survive or thrive if the temperature is too high or low; A warm-blooded animal is able to regulate its own temperature despite the surrounding temperature. However, what this presentation neglects is that the warm-blooded animal is also dependent on surroundings, just less so. A human survives only about three minutes in freezing water.

As social beings we are "warm-blooded." Although we can survive for a time without enough social support, we will not thrive indefinitely wouthout it. Our internalized sense of belonging can get us through periods of isolation,

---

Coping With Depression, Anxiety and Rage

The mind is its own place, and in itself
Can make a heaven of hell, a hell of heaven.
                    --John Milton (1608-1674)
                    Paradise Lost, Book I

There is nothing either good or bad, but thinking makes it so.
                    --William Shakespeare (1564-1616)
                    Hamlet, Act II, Scene ii

The five basic emotions are sadness, fear, anger, disgust, and happiness. Feeling happy is not a problem, and disgust is not a common problem. The extreme forms of the three remaining emotions _are_ common problems: depression, anxiety, and rage. Although this chapter guides you to multiple places to get support and education about how to cope with these feelings (and more complex ones as well), I also want to provide some basic coping information.

Cognitive-behavior therapy assumes that each feeling is connected to a thought. We cannot change feelings directly, but we can often change the thoughts connected to them, thereby changing the feeling. Sadness occurs when there are thoughts about having lost something. Fear occurs when we think there is danger. Anger occurs when we think we are being abused.

The first step in coping with these feelings is to evaluate the accuracy of the connected thought. Although we have thoughts all day, many of us do not understand basic facts about them. Thoughts occur effortlessly, but getting rid of them may not be easy (in this regard they are similar to cravings). Thoughts are not the same as beliefs (convictions built up over time). Thoughts come and go

but during these periods we need to be searching out new individuals and groups with whom to connect. Even the rugged individualists get together at times to congratulate each other on their independence.

In my early and lonely days of introducing to San Diego an alternative approach for addiction care, on occasion there was comfort and connection in reading a book by a colleague. Perhaps this workbook will bolster you until you find like-minded individuals. It is unwise to fit in just for the sake of doing so. Life is partly about finding the right peer groups for yourself. If you have them, nurture them. If not, keep looking.

Similarly, learning needs to be balanced between getting intensive guidance from a teacher, and being inquisitive and self-directed. If we insist on learning everything for ourselves, we will learn little because we lose out on the enormous efficiency of social learning. If we are always spoon fed knowledge by others, we won't develop our abilities to make the creative connections and discoveries that advance knowledge for everyone.

---

quickly. All thoughts "feel right" at first, and some are compelling. However, many thoughts are inaccurate or irrational. Only upon examination can we discover which ones are accurate and rational.

When sadness, concern and irritation, all feelings in the normal range, grow to depression, panic and rage, inaccurate thoughts are operating unchecked. Here are general guidelines for changing these thoughts and their related excessive emotions. First, the connection between the thought and the feeling needs to be established. ("I feel anxiety. What is the danger? I might be ridiculed.") Then the thought needs to be evaluated. There are two primary questions to consider. First, does the thought fit the evidence? ("These individuals have never ridiculed me before; I might be ridiculed but I don't know for sure that I will be; I sometimes think I am going to be ridiculed, but it rarely actually happens; One of these individuals likes me a great deal, so even if some ridiculed me not everybody would; If ridicule started, the individual who likes me would probably stand up for me, because that has happened before.") Second, is there a bigger perspective to consider? ("Even if I do get ridiculed, and even if my friend were not there to stick up for me, the consequences of this would be minor, really. I might feel bad for a while, but I would get over it quickly and there would be no permanent damage. I could tolerate it. I would also know that the individuals who ridiculed me may not be worth developing better friendships with.") Other questions might be considered as well, but these two can be used to evaluate most thoughts.

Addiction occurs because craving operates unchecked. Excessive emotion and emotional disorders occur because irrational thoughts go unchecked. By evaluating the true desirability of an addiction (by weighing both costs and benefits) and by evaluating the accuracy of thoughts (by examining the evidence pro and con and by considering bigger perspectives), you can know your true desires and beliefs. You need not be the victim of your cravings or your thoughts.

Questions . . .

1. In Chapter 4, Question 10, you provided a summary list of the current benefits of your addiction, and in Question 7 you checked off a complete list. These Questions asked you to identify what your addiction enables you to do. I suggested earlier that being able to do these things (being able to satisfy these needs) is in itself not a problem. It is not the end that is the problem, but the means. Review these answers now, to refresh your memory of what your addiction does for you. Summarize in your own words the primary coping methods that your addiction provides (you may simply be able to copy your answer to Chapter 4, Question 10):

2. Review your answers to the previous Question, and to Chapter 4, Question 9, which asks about whether you agree that these needs (which the addiction satisfies) are legitimate and worthwhile needs. If you are having a hard time concluding that they are legitimate, look deeper. For instance, a "need to get into trouble" may underneath be a "need to feel a thrill." A "need to be lazy" may underneath be a "need to relax or unwind." Is anything wrong with feeling an occasional thrill or relaxing? If you have not already done so for the Question above, describe your needs (that the addiction satisfies) in a way that you can feel good about:

3. We will detour a moment to recognize that even though your addiction has had costs, it has been *a* way to satisfy legitimate needs. Therefore, you could congratulate yourself for having found *a* way to satisfy them. During a famine you would congratulate yourself on finding any food, even if it were food you would not eat otherwise. What would your life had been like if you had found no way at all to satisfy these needs?

4. The first step to developing alternative coping methods has been taken. You have a list of needs to satisfy. You know what you are looking for. I mentioned earlier that it was likely that you have more than one addiction. It is even more likely that you have more than one need for which to find a new coping method. However, just as with the addictions, it may not be practical to develop several new coping methods simultaneously. It's time to prioritize. Write the alternative coping method(s) you would like to start developing first. You might choose this by focusing on the most pressing problem, or the coping method you think would be easiest to develop, or the coping method with the most readily available teaching help, or some other reason:

5. We learn any new knowledge or behavior by associating it with established knowledge and behavior. It will be useful to identify what you already know, and what you can already do (other than the addiction), to cope with the priority or priorities established in Question 4. If coping with something requires eight steps, you may already know six of them, and once you learn those last two, you are finished. This is much easier than needing to learn all eight. Describe the relevant knowledge and behavior that you already have:

6. Below is the list of ways to interact with others for the purpose of learning and experiencing social support. For each option, consider issues like cost, travel time, convenience, your own comfort level, and any other factors you consider relevant. For instance, the world's greatest psychotherapist won't be much good to you if she is very expensive, is far away, only works at times you cannot easily attend, and only provides nude hot tub group therapy (which you might not feel comfortable attending!). Consider the coping method at the top of your list in Question 4, and consider where you might like to learn about it, get support about it, or both. Place two checkmarks next to those options that seem highly appealing and likely to be helpful to you, one checkmark next to options you would consider, and no marks for those you are uninterested in.

___reading

___audiotapes or radio

___videotapes or television

___a play or movie

___a lecture

___a class

___a support or discussion group

___a professionally led educational group

___group psychotherapy

___individual coaching or instruction

___individual or couples psychotherapy or counseling

___discussion with trusted others

___discussion with acquaintances

___observing any good model

___doing any of the above, in imagination

___other options

7. What is the best self-help book you have read? What did you learn from it? How helpful would it be to review that book again?

8. If you could participate in a weekly or monthly informal group discussion about any subject at all, what would that subject be?

 9. What changes could you make in your own communication behavior that might improve your close relationships? Are there any specific changes needed for specific relationships?

10. What groups would you like to become a member of (these could be formal organizations, or informal groups like the "in" crowd)? What would it take to become recognized as a member?

11. What groups that you are not a member of could you make a significant contribution to? How satisfying would it be to make this contribution?

12. Remember that you already have a track record (my apologies to the gamblers) of learning new information and behaviors in your life, and in particular you have learned a number of coping methods. As Question 5 above notes, you probably don't need to learn "everything" about your new coping method, only parts of it. You have done it before; you can do it again. Just to emphasize this point (and build your self-confidence), let's activate some coping memories. List at least three types of situations in which you cope well. If you are having a hard time remembering them, recall when others have told you things like "you did a good job on that":

13. Rather than aiming at perfection in the development of your new coping method, "good enough" is a reasonable initial goal. Later you can continue to improve. In Question 4 you identified a coping method to learn more about. How confident are you that this new coping method, if you do it "well enough," would work as well as the addiction? How long will it take to learn this new coping method "well enough"? Besides no longer needing the addiction, and no longer suffering its costs, do you expect any other advantages to using the new coping method instead of the addiction? How do you compare the costs of the new coping method with the costs of the addiction?

14. What other coping methods will you need to learn for the addiction not to be missed greatly?

15. If you have more than one answer to Question 4, place them in the best order to learn them. Then next to each coping method write the way or ways of interacting with others that you would prefer to rely on for assistance (using Question 6 as a guide).

16. To what extent has being isolated contributed to your addiction starting or continuing? What would be your ideal peer group? How could you come close to having it?

17. Review your answers to the second half of Question 13, Chapter 4. Do any of these answers now seem irrational to you? Why?

Projects . . .

---

1. Review the checkmarks on the list in Question 6 above, and select one or more of the interactions as a place to start. Report back here after your first contact. What did you learn? How much connection did you feel to the other or others you were with?

2. For one week, at least twice each day, "reach out" and connect with others, once to receive support or information, and once to give it. These efforts can occur with individuals you know or those new to you. How satisfying are these efforts? Is it easier to give or receive?

3. Compare this Project to Project 2, Chapter 2. Identify the most supportive person you have ever known. If possible, have a conversation with this individual. If it is not possible (e.g., this person is no longer alive), have the conversation in imagination. If you having difficulty identifying a very supportive person, imagine a conversation with me. Tell this person the history of your problems with addiction, and describe the steps you think are needed to overcome the addiction. How does it feel to say all this? What do you learn?

4. If there is an alternative support group in your area, attend one meeting. How did it go?

5. If there is not an alternative support group in your area, investigate these groups, select the one best suited to you, and start your own meeting. The best way to learn something is to teach it! How satisfying is it to initiate and lead your own meeting?

6. Review your answer to Question 8 above. If there is a subject that you would like to talk about with others, contact others with similar interests and start some informal way of staying in touch with one another, possibly even a group meeting. How satisfying is it to initiate increased communication?

What's Important Now?

(If you date your answers to these questions, the answers over time will become a diary of your growth. It is likely that in future readings of this chapter different ideas will be important to you, reflecting the fact that you are indeed changing)

Which ideas from this chapter are most useful *to you, now*?

How can you put these ideas into action?

How much confidence do you have in your judgement in selecting these ideas as crucial at this time? (Circle a number; 10 is highest confidence)

0   1   2   3   4   5   6   7   8   9   10

You Have Choices

7

There are three ways to get something done:
Do it yourself, hire someone to do it,
or forbid your kids to do it.

Overview

You don't *have to* overcome your addiction or change it in any way. You have
choices. You have no choice about dying or certain bodily processes. You do
have choice about almost everything else (even if you don't like the options
available). Others may say that you "have to" change or stop your addiction, but
you don't. If you are told this, the resentment you feel in response may become a
problem for you. Either cutting back (moderation) or stopping altogether
(abstinence) can be successful ways to overcome your addiction. Success with
either will depend on your preferences, circumstances, and capacity for self-
control, among other factors. Your life will probably be happier if your day-to-
day choices are based on your long-term goals and ultimate values.

Making Choices, But Not Necessarily Liking the Options

There are many activities or changes that might be highly desirable and valuable for you, but you don't have to do them. You have a choice about them. For instance, it might be quite valuable to your health and your relationships to overcome your addiction. However, other individuals with similar levels of addiction have not changed. You, too, could continue with the addiction, regardless of how self-destructive it is.

One major aspect of life that none of us has a choice about is death. As far as we know, there is ultimately no way to prevent death. What lives must die. It is not something anyone has a choice about. Similarly, there are certain bodily functions that happen regardless of whether we want them to. Most everything else in life involves a choice, so it's not correct to say, "I *must* overcome my addiction."

It commonly occurs that we don't like the choices that face us. If the car I want to buy comes with a price tag I don't want to pay, I don't like my options (no new car or pay the high price). I may attempt to discover some creative additional options, but probably these will have their own advantages and disadvantages as well. Ultimately, it's my choice, and I (and others) will live with the consequences of my choice.

Not all choices are made in a thoughtful and rational manner, of course, nor would it be desirable for them to be. There are many decisions in life for which guidelines such as "what's easiest" or "what's good enough" or "what's quickest" are better than "what's best." It would be desirable, however, if *major decisions* were made in a careful, rational manner. A cost-benefit analysis, which we just conducted in Chapters 3 through 5, is an example of a careful, rational decision-making process.

Through such a rational process you can decide on a course of action even when you might prefer to have other options. The option that you might prefer is to have a "perfect addiction," as described in Chapter 5 -- one with no costs. This option is not available, at least for now.

This chapter will help you identify some broad options for overcoming your addiction. Some of these options might be considered "creative solutions," and you might not have been aware that they existed. Ultimately, however, there is a limited range of options, and you will choose between them, even if you choose to do nothing differently than you have been doing.

There Are Many Self-Appointed Experts About Addiction

Some individuals, in an effort to be helpful to you, may emphasize how important it is for you to change your addiction. They may say "you have to stop." Although this is probably meant to be helpful, it is actually not helpful. Almost anyone, when told "you have to do this, you must stop, you can't continue," or similar statements, experiences some degree of resentment or rebelliousness. Some individuals experience these feelings very strongly. You may already be experiencing enough difficulties attempting to change your addiction. If you also need to cope with resentment and rebelliousness, overcoming addiction just gets harder.

Remember: *you don't have to do anything* (except die); *you have a choice*. If someone says that you have to change, you could reply that you don't *have to* change, you are choosing to change. You might also say that you don't have to change, but you need to change in order to accomplish goals that are important to you. Even if you don't persuade that individual that you have a choice (it's hard to change self-appointed experts), you'll probably feel better for having made a response.

Another advantage of this recognition of choice is that it is difficult to take credit for doing something you *have* to do, but the credit is completely yours if you *choose* to do it. You will probably feel better about choosing to change, and getting credit for it, rather than having to change, and not getting credit.

Even if someone does not recognize that changing an addiction is a choice, not a "have to," their lack of recognition does not change the situation. Facts are facts. Regardless of what anyone else thinks, *it's up to you* what happens with your addiction.

There are three important variations on being told that you "have to" change your addiction. It is possible for one "part" of you to think "I have to change" and another part to be resentful of this command. It is the same situation as before, only you play both roles. This variation can be harder to cope with because there is no outsider to recognize and argue against. I have heard many individuals say that they now realize they have to change. What they mean is that they now understand deeply that they don't want any more negative consequences, and that these negative consequences are going to keep happening if they stay involved with the addiction. The short way to say this is that they *need* to change (in order not to suffer more). But they still can go on with the addiction if they change their minds!

A second variation is telling yourself (or hearing from outside) that you must "never" engage in the addiction again. This arouses both resentment, as we just described, and fear. The fear is that someday you may need or deeply want your addiction again, but because of a prior decision it won't be available to you. But there is no prior decision (with a few dramatic exceptions) that will stop you from engaging in the addiction later if you change your mind. The fear and resentment build up, and a slip or relapse may occur. Over time, the notion of "never" may grow comfortable to you, but that probably won't happen for a long time. By the time "never" feels comfortable, it's probably not needed. Saying "never" is not a good substitute for gaining experience without the addiction, and it may make gaining that experience more difficult.

An additional aspect about "never" is that it is usually suggested, either by yourself or others, in the aftermath of a crisis ("You just lost at that card room all the money we had saved for vacation: You must never gamble again!"). Do you recall having an addiction crisis? It includes confusion, fear, anger, conflict with others, efforts to cope with consequences, and possibly many other factors. During a crisis you are not in a state of mind to make a permanent decision about anything! A temporary plan to get you past the crisis seems more sensible. You can make longer term plans later.

A third variation involves feeling deprived and resentful. If you think that you "must" change your addiction, and you are around others who still engage in that behavior, you may feel depirved ("these people can still do this, but I can't anymore"). Feeling deprived can lead to feeling resentful, and that in turn can lead back to addiction. The accurate way to describe this situation is that others may not experience the negatives that you experience from the addiction (or they may!), but you are choosing to change because you want the benefits of change. Rather than focusing on what you are "deprived" of by changing, you can shift your focus to what you will gain by it.

The Change Some 12-Step Supporters Need To Make

I accept that many 12-step supporters are completely devoted to the 12-step philosophy. When something appears to have saved you (or others), loyalty is natural. What I don't accept willingly is anyone being told that the 12 steps are the *only* way to overcome addiction.

Imagine someone in the midst of the crises that arise from addiction. This person may reach out to some trusted individual or authority for guidance. In many situations of this type in the U.S., the individual seeking guidance is referred to AA. AA attendance may be the primary or only suggestion made. Imagine this individual attending an AA meeting and for any number of reasons not resonating to the approach. This individual persists, however, because the recommendation to AA came from a trusted source. After a while, however, despite a diligent effort, this individual realizes that, however effective AA may be for others, it is not working personally.

What might this individual be told, when this realization is voiced? Perhaps the response is: "There are other approaches. Maybe one of them would work better for you. The important thing is to overcome your addiction. How you do it is not the issue. If the other approaches don't help either, you could come back to AA. Maybe things would be different then, and AA might be more suitable for you. But maybe another approach will work. Most of all we just hope you are successful."

Perhaps the response is: "You fail to realize how personally incompetent you are, and this failure just confirms your incompetence. You cannot hope to recover on your own, without a higher power. You are not opening your heart to receive your higher power. You are trying to decide what is best for yourself. Only your higher power can show you that. Unless you accept this willfulness as an expression of your character defects and of the insanity of your disease, you are lost."

I hope that the first response would happen always. My experience suggests that the second response is common. It is offered by a presumably well-meaning 12-step supporter. Many individuals might receive it and just ignore it. They may intuitively understand that even though they are being blamed, the problem is not with themselves but with the mismatch between themselves and the 12 steps. I am concerned about the vulnerable, self-doubting individual, in the midst of addictive crisis, who is not able to rise above the personal criticism to see this mismatch. For such individuals there is significant possibility of emotional damage. If the individual does not know that alternatives exist (and many do not), the individual does not seek them out. For some individuals receiving such criticism leads back to addiction. Depression or suicide are also possibilities.

In reality there are many ways to overcome addiction. AA is one of them. It is not the only one. Saying otherwise is potentially a disastrous disservice to some individuals. I hope that this disservice fades away quickly.

To Abstain or Moderate: Factors to Consider

So far I have talked about overcoming or changing addiction, but I have not mentioned "abstinence." This workbook assumes that the choice between moderation or abstinence is a highly personal one, and that many factors will be involved in making the choice. I will review these factors and provide guidance on choosing between stopping altogether or just cutting back. It will usually be wise not to make a permanent decision (a "never") until you have significant experience with one or both. Therefore, the following considerations are intended to help you choose between a trial of moderation or a trial of abstinence. Once you have more experience you will be in position to evaluate your success and make longer term plans. Factors to consider include:

⇒ your level of *motivation* for each option

⇒ your current *circumstances*

⇒ your capacity for and beliefs about *self-control*

⇒ whether you are ready for the *work* and *decision-making* required to moderate
     successfully

⇒ whether the addiction is *legal or illegal*

⇒ your *past successes* abstaining or moderating

⇒ how serious *the next slip* or relapse might be

⇒ what *significant others* in your life would prefer (spouse, family, friends,
    behavioral health professionals)

⇒ what *authorities* with power over you might be insisting on (probation
    officer, licensing board, employer)

◆ **Motivation.** A major advantage of moderation is that you may be much more motivated to moderate than to abstain. Unfortunately, moderation can gradually (and sometimes not so gradually) become excess. If this is happening, you can *tell* yourself that you are moderating, but what you have really done is cut back to a less but still harmful level (or possibly not even that). By moderation I mean a level of involvement that has no significant costs. That level will be different for different individuals and depends on a large number of factors. Cutting back to a lower level of harm (harm reduction) is movement in the right direction, and better than no movement at all, but it is not moderation.

    It is commonly feared that individuals with severe addiction will unrealistically hope that they can be moderators. However, most individuals with severe addictions choose, at least when they enter treatment, to abstain. On the other hand, many with mild to moderate problems prefer to attempt moderation, and this option often seems worth a try.

    For now there is insufficient research to guide a professional in recommending moderation or abstinence. The individual's motivation appears to be the most important factor. You may have heard that those with severe problems are less likely than those with mild or moderate problems to moderate. This is true and would appear to be an argument against moderating. What is left out of this argument is that those with severe problems are also less likely to abstain. The important issue is not moderation or abstinence, but the severity of the problem. Fortunately, if your motivation is high, either solution can occur.

◆ **Circumstances.** I believe that anyone can moderate any addiction, given the right circumstances. As a practical matter, getting the right circumstances may not be feasible or worth the effort. For instance, imagine yourself at one of the worst periods of your addiction, when the cravings seemed irresistible and the costs of the addiction were mounting dramatically. Now imagine that I enter the scene, just as you are about to engage in the addiction one more time (take another drink, break open another pound of chocolates, light another cigarette, roll the dice one more time, etc.). I have a loaded gun. I hold it to your head. I say, "Do it and you die."

What are the chances you would continue with your addiction? If you did, we would say, not that you were addicted, but that you were suicidal!

This scenario highlights the existence of choice in addiction. When faced with strong enough immediate consequences, anyone can stop or cut back. Under normal circumstances, however, there is usually some "wiggle room" about the consequences. How strong will they actually be? Can I reduce them somehow? How immediate will they be? In the gun-to-the-head scenario, the answers to these questions are clear. Under normal circumstances, the choice to act on the addiction is an expression of the (mistaken) belief "I can get away with it this time." With a gun to your head, you know you can't get away with it this time.

It's not practical to hire an assassin to follow you around all day (although it would work if you did!). However, sometimes other protective factors can easily be arranged and are often helpful in the early stages of change. For instance, you can be accompanied by someone who will support you, avoid certain people or places or activities, or substitute other substances or activities for the addictive one (e.g., chewing on a straw instead of smoking, having a glass of juice instead of a glass of wine, going dancing instead of gambling, a cold shower instead of sex).

For some individuals, however, it can be difficult to arrange for these protective factors. There may be no suitable companion for critical times, temptations may be frequent, friends may actually encourage continued involvement with the addiction, and alternative coping methods may still be weak. All of these problems are difficult enough to deal with when abstaining, but they can be even more difficult when attempting to moderate. This increased difficulty with moderation occurs because cravings are often stronger after one has engaged in the addiction a little, than if one had abstained to start with.

You are reading this workbook (if it is for yourself) because your involvement with some substance or activity is excessive, and this excess occurred because of acting on craving. During each episode of addiction craving continues past the point of moderation, and so do you. If you weren't going past the point of moderation, you wouldn't, by definition, have an addiction. For you, then, trying to stop at the point of moderation will leave you experiencing a craving, and one that is probably stronger than the one that started that episode. In attempting to moderate you will end up feeling worse (with respect to craving) than when you began that episode. This is not bad in itself, nor is it impossible to deal with (see Chapters 8, 9 and 10).

One of the ways to deal with craving is to arrange circumstances to protect you. If you are unable to do this very well, then *increasing* your craving by attempting to moderate may increase the probability of lack of success, as compared to just abstaining. In this way moderation could be compared to drinking salt water to quench thirst. The more you drink, the thirstier you get. To a great extent we control ourselves by controlling our circumstances. If you can't easily control other circumstances, then abstinence may be your path to overcoming addiction.

◆ **Self-control**. Fortunately, in addition to controlling circumstances, there is another route to increased self-control. That route involves the evaluation and development of one's goals and values. In order to demonstrate how this is true, I need to explain a remarkable fact about addiction.

Regardless of how severe someone's addiction is, even if it is a seemingly hopeless case, the addicted individual still limits to a degree his or her involvement with the addiction. Even though we might be tempted to describe this individual as "out of control," a degree of control is always being used. For instance, consider the two-pack-a-day mother who won't smoke around her kids, the 12-beers-a-day man who won't drink at work, the gambler who will not go to the casino when Mom is visiting, the homeless person who will not steal from a charity (in order to buy street drugs), the coke user who craves more but won't pawn personal possessions to get more money, the sex addict who won't touch anyone in his family.

Each of these individuals is demonstrating a degree of control, although not a large enough degree to prevent negative consequences from the addiction. Unfortunately, this extremely important fact about addiction is typically overlooked in discussions of addiction as a "disease characterized by loss of control." The definition of "alcoholism" written jointly by the American Society of Addiction Medicine and the National Council on Alcoholism and Drug

Dependence does in its most recent revision (1990) substitute the term "impaired control" for "loss of control," but the U.S. addiction treatment industry seems not to have incorporated this change in its public presentations.

How is it that these out-of-control individuals actually have a degree of control? This control occurs because they have not completely lost sight of their goals or values. They could increase control by connecting even more with these goals and values. That connection is the foundation of any type of self-control.

To paraphrase Aristotle again, the ultimate aim in life is happiness. It is the end which we all seek. An ultimate goal is (what we think is) the last step before happiness ("I want to be rich, because if I'm rich, I'll be happy"). Other goals point to ultimate goals. Values are the guidelines and preferences we live by ("I'm going to be rich, but I'm going to do it honestly"). The myriad levels of goals, values, habits and other behaviors and beliefs are different levels of means to the ultimate end of happiness.

One of the most vivid examples I have seen of the idea of degrees of control occurred when I treated a heroin addict. Heroin is expensive, and if injected, it is often used daily. Holding a job and injecting heroin daily is a juggling act not everyone can manage. Consequently, many heroin addicts steal. The woman I was treating might have stolen from me if I had not kept close watch on her. By traditional concepts she was clearly "out of control." But she told me that despite her extensive history of theft, she had never stolen from her family. This fact was a matter of pride to her, but not, so it seemed to me, in a boastful way. She was proud because she valued her family enough not to abuse them, even though she had been tempted to do so many times. She knew her own value on this matter, and this value guided her behavior, even though a sacrifice was required.

To know one's own values, and to let them guide behavior, even if sacrifice is involved: this is a recipe for overcoming addiction. It may even be a recipe for happiness.

When we speak of capacity for self-control, we are referring to the degree of practice someone has acting on deeper values, and moving toward ultimate goals, despite the sacrifices involved. If you have significant self-control in areas other than addiction, it may not be that difficult to transfer this capacity to overcoming addiction. If you completed the cost-benefit analysis in Chapters 3, 4 and 5, you may have recognized that this might also have been called a *values clarification* exercise. If your values as they relate to addiction were clarified in those chapters, you may have seen a clear contradiction between your values and your behavior. Perhaps the only elements that might still be in the way of your overcoming addiction are the degree of sacrifice you expect to be required, and your confidence in your ability to cope with that degree of sacrifice.

For some individuals sacrifice is not a way of life. For these individuals the notion of loss of control is often appealing, and the notion of stopping after a little bit of involvement doesn't really make much sense to them. This is another time to be honest with yourself. If you know now that your plans for moderation will disappear once you start, wouldn't it be better to abstain? Perhaps once you are clearer about your goals and values, you will be in a better position to moderate.

◆ **Decision-making**. A major advantage of abstinence is simplicity. You don't need to decide how much addictive involvement to have; you just stop. A related advantage is that after several months of abstinence, cravings typically go away altogether, or nearly so (see Chapters 8-10). If you are moderating, this evaporation of craving may not occur as fully. With each craving you are faced with another decision. Abstinence simplifies your life.

If you are going to moderate, here are some general guidelines to consider. There is considerable decision-making effort beyond what abstinence would require.

1. Make initial plans about how much involvement to have. At what times? Under what circumstances (with whom, where, why)? At what pace (e.g., if you are aiming to drink moderately, it is wise to pace your drinking by sipping instead of gulping, spacing your sips, and alternating with non-alcoholic beverages). Consider a planned gradual reduction in involvement, if moderation immediately does not seem realistic. If moderation (involvement but no significant costs) is not the eventual goal, how do you justify this decision? Of course, only you can define what significant costs are, but if you think you are paying significant costs for your addiction, isn't it time to find some other ways to meet your needs?

2. Keep a record of your involvement by carrying a small notebook with you. You need this record to keep yourself honest, and to protect against the normal lapses of human memory. A simpler recording method would be to make a once daily note on a calendar.

3. Seek out and arrange for protective factors. This means arranging circumstances that will help you follow through with your plans (have a suitable companion, only have access to so much or for only so long, avoid certain places or people, etc.)

4. Consider moderation to be an experiment. Switch to abstinence, or get professional help, if the experiment is not working well. As a rough guideline, *if*

there is not complete or major success within one to three months, abstinence or a major revision of your plans is indicated. On the other hand, if your attempts at moderation are disastrous from the beginning, you might end the experiment within days.

5. If in doubt about the level of involvement, err on the side of underinvolvement. Remember that "moderation" can include a level of involvement that might more accurately be called "near abstinence." The sense of freedom from such a plan can be enormous. If you hate the thought of abstinence, but shudder at following through on the steps just outlined, near abstinence might be for you. For instance, you could choose to engage in your addiction only a few times throughout the year (e.g., once a quarter, certain holidays, certain vacations, your birthday, etc.).

6. Include all other aspects of overcoming addiction, as discussed elsewhere in this workbook. In one sense abstinence and moderation are identical. Both involve stopping, just at different points. Therefore, reward yourself frequently (especially at first), identify and develop alternative coping methods, cope with craving, refuse offers to be over-involved with the substance or activity, recognize triggers and high risk situations in order to prevent relapse, and get support from others for changing.

◆ **Legal or illegal?** By mentioning the possibility that you would moderate or reduce your involvement with illegal substances or activities, I do not mean to recommend engaging in illegal acts. I am aware, however, that many individuals are simply unwilling to abstain. I hope that the ideas and techniques in this workbook will help you reduce the negative consequences of your addiction, even if your plan is not to abstain altogether. Perhaps once you reach a reduced level, abstinence will not seem so undesirable or unreachable.

It is worth reminding you that the negative consequences of arrest for illegal addictive activity can be horrendous (e.g., very long prison terms, large fines, large legal fees, loss of a professional and/or driving license). This activity can also lead to irreparable harm to others (e.g., crashing into someone when drunk driving; becoming paranoid and violent when on stimulants).

◆ **Past successes**. In general the best predictor of the future is the past. Your history of success or difficulty with abstinence or moderation will suggest your likelihood of success in the future. Your history may also suggest what you need to do differently. Past difficulties do not necessarily indicate future difficulties. What past difficulty shows is where it is likely to occur again if a new approach is not developed. Those who persist in efforts to overcome addiction will likely be successful, provided they persist mindfully.

Persisting mindfully may include deciding to abstain. Imagine that you have run an experiment multiple times, and each time you get the same result. You don't want that result, but you can think of no new ways to run the experiment. It's time to face reality. It is likely that the next time you run the experiment the same way, you will get the same result. If no new ideas are available for running the experiment (a professional consult might be helpful here), maybe it's time to try a different experiment.

◆ **The next slip**. One of the difficulties with traditional treatment's almost-exclusive focus on abstinence is the difficulty acknowledging that changing an addiction is, like most other learning, a trial-and-error process. Rather than accepting error as part of the process of change, it is usually considered part of the addiction.

Almost everyone attempting to change an addiction has one or more slips, which we could also call difficulty following through completely. A prolonged slip is called a relapse, and these are not uncommon either. Better to recognize and accept this, and plan for it, than to blindly hope it just won't happen. These difficulties could be called failures, but that description would ignore what has already been stated. You already have a degree of control over your addiction, and that degree needs to be improved. You weren't even a failure before you started changing. By making the effort to change, even if you are having difficulty, you are better off than before you started.

Consider your risk of slips and relapses if you aim to moderate, and if you aim to abstain. Is there a significant difference between them? It may be difficult to know the answer to this question. I remind you, however, of the possibility that craving will be stronger if you attempt to moderate, and that difficulty coping with craving got you to this point.

Consider also the consequences of your next slip or relapse. If your spouse is ready to leave you, your employer ready to fire your, your probation officer ready to incarcerate you, or your liver ready to give out on you, wouldn't it make sense to err on the safe side? Calculation of risk includes the consequences of failure as well as the likelihood of failure. If the consequences of failure could be disastrous, the risk is high, even when the likelihood of failure is relatively low. I don't normally just fall over when I am standing up, but when I am standing next to a large, fatal drop off, I am much more cautious about losing my balance than when I am standing in the middle of a large trampoline. Don't set yourself up to fall off the edge!

◆ **Significant others.** Abstinence may be more acceptable to those around you, who may have good reason to fear that you will not be successful at moderation. One way to negotiate an agreement about this is to suggest a *trial* of moderation, monitored by your significant other. If you do this trial, it is advisable to get this individual to agree not to convey verbal or non-verbal disapproval of your moderated addictive involvement, to agree in advance on the consequences of slips, and to agree in advance on how success or failure will be judged and how each will be handled. You need to feel free to enjoy your involvement, but also to know what the consequences will be if you go beyond moderation.

Professionals, either behavioral health professionals generally or addiction treatment professionals in particular, are not "significant others" in the usual sense of this term. However, while you are involved with them they can be quite significant in your life. What about considering their preferences regarding moderation or abstinence?

In the United States (although not in most other parts of the world) moderation versus abstinence has been one of the most controversial issues in the field of addiction treatment. Almost all U.S. treatment programs tell the client to abstain, without consideration of what the client is motivated to do.

I believe that this is overstepping a professional's role. Here's an analogy: If you entered couples therapy, you would not expect the therapist to tell you whether to split up or stay together. It would be presumptuous of the therapist to give either opinion. It is *impossible* to know someone well enough to make a truly informed recommendation. It is the therapist's role to help you improve your relationship. Regardless of any recommendation you would receive, each partner in the relationship will ultimately decide if the improvement is sufficient to stay together.

I believe that a professional should aim to help you eliminate or at least reduce the costs of your addiction. It's up to you to decide how much reduction is enough. When a professional and a client argue about moderation versus abstinence, it provides one more opportunity for the client to feel resentful, and it takes time away from the other issues the client needs to work on. The resentment is unnecessary, and it gets in the way of learning new behavior. It may even drive the client away from getting help altogether (by "abstaining" from treatment). Moderating or abstaining is a tactical decision in service of the goal of eliminating or reducing addictive costs. If a bad decision has been made, the consequences will be apparent, and the client can make a different decision.

It *is* a professional's job to restate priorities, facts and probabilities. This may appear to be stating a recommendation, but it is not. For instance, I might say: "Based on what I have heard your partner say, if you adopt a moderation plan, your partner will leave. For now getting your partner to see it differently doesn't look likely. If keeping your relationship together is your highest priority, which is what you told me last week, then it looks like abstinence is the way to go for you, at least for now. Am I wrong about any of this?" Or, "Your physician told you that if you drink even small amounts, your liver will get even worse. If it does get worse, she expects your life expectancy to be months, not years. If living awhile longer is important to you, and you said it was, then it appears that abstinence is what you want to do. Did I miss anything?"

An addiction changes when you understand that costs exceed benefits (and understand what to do to change). If you are slow to grasp the facts and probabilities of the situation, the professional is not required to act dumb. Sometimes a simple restatement of facts and probabilities, and a confirmation of your stated priorities, can help you experience a "blinding flash of the obvious." These flashes can be pertinent to the choice of moderation or abstinence, or the broader issue of overcoming addiction.

A professional recommendation that goes against your perception of facts and probabilities, not to mention your priorities, is unlikely to change your mind. If the (probably longstanding) negative consequences of the addiction have not persuaded you to abstain, how is a new and relatively unknown professional going to succeed in persuading you in that direction? If the two of you are far apart on the perception of facts, coming to some common ground would appear to be the place to start. Keep in mind that you are on ground that the professional has been on many times, so giving the professional the benefit of the doubt on some issues is often appropriate. However, suggesting that you *definitely* can or cannot be successful at moderating or abstaining is going beyond anyone's power to predict outcome, given the present state of knowledge. There are self-appointed experts even among professionals.

Ironically, moderation goals are even included in 12-step programs, but the description of them conceals this. In Overeaters Anonymous members aim to abstain from overeating (but not all eating!). In Sexaholics Anonymous, Sexual Compulsives Anonymous, and Sex and Love Addicts Anonymous some sexual experiences are accepted, and others are to be abstained from. The latter two groups allow their members to make their own definition of abstinence, which of course could also be described as a definition of moderation.

◆ **Authorities.** Your addiction may have brought you into contact with the law. Courts and their representatives, and professional licensing boards, almost always favor abstinence plans. Although you still have the choice about whether to comply with an abstinence plan, these bodies can apply highly unpleasant consequences if you fail to comply. As stated before, it's still your choice, but you may not like the options. One perspective to consider is that these authorities have only time-limited coercive authority over you.

To Abstain or Moderate?

What's your decision? We have reviewed factors to consider when deciding between a trial of moderation or a trial of abstinence, but you may still be unsure about what to do. It is remarkable that when my clients are obviously unsure about this choice, they still do not *ask* for a recommendation. However, I am willing to suggest (for you or for them) a temporary period of abstinence. Make the period short enough that you are confident you can succeed (a few days, a week, a month). If you have some experience stopping, you might choose a longer period, even up to a year or two. At the end of the time period, you can renew it, commit to permanent abstinence, or attempt moderation. A period of abstinence is often valuable for clearing out the negative effects of the addiction, and this usually results in clearer thinking. For this reason temporary abstinence is a good way to begin a moderation plan also.

If you are a substance user who might experience withdrawal symptoms if you stop suddenly (or if you are not sure about whether you will), see the sidebar on "medications and overcoming addiction" on page 170. Knowing about withdrawal may save you much discomfort and could possibly save your life!

In summary, I am encouraging you to attempt the approach (moderation or abstinence) that appears to be most sensible for you, to change if your first approach does not seem to be working, and to keep changing and trying as necessary until you succeed. Research has discovered that some individuals can moderate, some can abstain, and many unfortunately can apparently do neither. With luck even these nonmoderating individuals will at least cut back. At this time there are no methods for predicting accurately which individuals will succeed with abstinence or moderation, which will cut back, and which will continue as before or worse. For now your own motivation and experience are your most important guides for deciding about these issues.

The goal is to stop experiencing the negative consequences of addiction. If abstinence or moderation gets you there, that's what counts! It's your life. You get the rewards, you pay the consequences, you decide! Even if you are only partly successful, you are better off. In time perhaps you will be more successful.

Having Day-to-Day Choices Be Consistent With Ultimate Goals and Deeply Held Values

If you know well what you truly want in life, and what you truly value, then day-to-day choices are much easier to make. The chances are also good that if you know what you want and value, then you will decide that addiction does not fit in your life. Addiction interferes with long-term goals and values. One cannot serve well too many masters. We will return to these issues again in later chapters.

Questions . . .

1. Do you truly have a choice about continuing with your addiction, or do you *have to* change? Explain your perspective:

2. When others tell you that you *have to* stop your addiction, or that you *have to* change it, how do you feel? What do you say in return? How often are you told these things? Do you experience any differences when different individuals say these things? Do significant others have any other thoughts about what you should do?

3. Recall one or more major decisions that you have made. To what extent did these decisions seem like choices you freely made (even if you didn't like the options)? To what extent, as you made these decisions, did you believe others were placing you in a position in which you did not want to be?

4. To what extent is resentment a troublesome feeling for you? How do you compare your typical level of resentment, and your typical ability to deal with it, to that of others? (You might also check Question 6 in Chapter 3 and Question 7 in Chapter 4, to see if in either place you checked "to rebel" as a benefit of addiction. If so resentment may be significant issue for you.)

5. To what extent do you feel that others inappropriately try to control you? To what extent did your parents or guardians inappropriately try to control you?

6. If you have reached a decision regarding a trial of abstinence or a trial of moderation, which is it? Why?

7. Regardless of whether you are planning to abstain or moderate, or don't yet know, what circumstances in your life could you adjust to help you succeed?

8. How much do you believe that once you start to engage in your addiction it is impossible to stop? Explain your perspective:

9. Have you had episodes of being "out of control"? Recall one. How did this episode end? What is the reason you did not continue in this episode longer? Could you have continued longer if you had been highly motivated to? For instance, suppose I had come along and motivated you by offering you something highly desirable ("I will pay you one million dollars," "I will give you the man/woman of your dreams," "I will make you a master of any ability you choose," etc.). Would you have been able to persist in your addiction for one more hour? Do you recall other occasions of being "out of control" when these motivators might have influenced you to continue past the point you stopped?

10. List your past successes moderating or abstaining (you answered a similar question in Chapter 2, Question 5). What have you learned from each of these experiences that you can now apply to overcoming your addiction?

11. List your past difficulties with moderating or abstaining. What have you learned from each of these experiences that you can now apply to overcoming your addiction?

12. If you have begun or are about to begin an abstinence or moderation plan, what are the most likely ways in which a slip could occur? What might turn a slip into a relapse? How serious might the consequences of a slip or relapse be?

13. If you have begun or are about to begin an abstinence or moderation plan, how likely are you to be successful? What are the reasons for your confidence or lack of confidence?

14. How likely are you to have significant withdrawal symptoms if you stop your addiction suddenly?

15. What are your ultimate goals in life?

16. What sub-goals are needed to be in position to accomplish these ultimate goals? For instance, if you want to be a psychologist you need to get accepted to college, graduate, get accepted to graduate school, etc.

17. What are your most deeply held values?

18. To what extent would keeping in mind these goals and values help you to follow through on a plans to overcome addiction?

Projects . . .

1. Pay attention to how often you use phrases like "I have to, I can't, I must, I've got to." Each time you say or are tempted to say one of these phrases, substitute "I need to," or "I would be better off if I..." (Unless you are talking about dying or some bodily processes, "I need to" is accurate and the others are not). You may think that this change of wording is not worth working on, that it is meaningless, that it is a "matter of semantics." The question this Project asks, however, is whether you experience an emotional difference when you change from "I have to" to "I need to." When you make this change, what happens? How often do you have occasion to make this change?

2. If in Question 4 above you identified resentment as a recurring troublesome problem for you, keep a *resentment log* for the coming week. Record the date/time, resentment on a 0 to 10 scale, and the situation or persons involved. What patterns do you notice? To what extent do you think resentment is a significant problem for you?

3. You have identified your ultimate goal, sub-goals and deeply held values. For the next week, take at least one action every day that puts into practice one goal and one value. Notice how you feel as you do this project. To what extent does this project feel like a burden?

4. If you are ready, write out your plans for overcoming addiction. If you are ready, put these plans into effect. What do you learn from acting on these plans?

What's Important Now?

If you date your answers to these Questions, the answers over time will become a diary of your growth. It is likely that in future readings of this chapter different ideas will be important to you, reflecting the fact that you are indeed changing.

Which ideas from this chapter are most useful *to you, now*?

How can you put these ideas into action?

How much confidence do you have in your judgement in selecting these ideas as crucial at this time? (Circle a number; 10 is highest confidence)

0   1   2   3   4   5   6   7   8   9   10

8

Identifying Craving

Some have too much, yet still do crave.
                    -- Sir Edward Dyer (1543-1607)

Overview

Craving to engage in your addiction occurs at times. You experience craving because you have had repeated experience with your addiction. The craving will subside over time if your experience ends. Monitoring craving is a simple way to understand it better. Craving is partly predictable.

Craving is a function of experience

Consider hunger. Hunger is a state of tension and discomfort that motivates you to eat. When hungry, your attention shifts increasingly to thoughts about food. You may grow irritable. Your stomach may "growl." You may feel lightheaded.

Hunger is a complete (cognitive, emotional, and physical) experience. As time passes it becomes an increasingly uncomfortable one. Once we eat enough, of course, hunger goes away. Hunger's motivational task is complete, for the moment. When your body is ready for more food, hunger will arise again. Similarly, we experience urges to drink liquids (thirst) and cravings for sexual experience (feeling "turned on," to use just one of many expressions for sexual craving).

I am focusing here on physical hunger, which any animal experiences, but ignoring food cravings associated with a food addiction. Food cravings (such as for chocolate) arise for primarily psychological reasons, not physical ones. They are related to hunger, but not identical to it.

Do you recall how little you may have eaten when you experienced no hunger, perhaps because you were sick or upset? Although we can eat when not hungry, typically we do not eat as much, nor enjoy it as much. Cancer and other medical patients often need to push themselves to eat. Eating provides little satisfaction for them, even though they may clearly need the food.

Craving (or an urge), like hunger, thirst, and sexual craving, is a state of tension that motivates you to engage in your addiction. Craving is uncomfortable, and it is motivating because it is uncomfortable. By engaging in the addiction you make the craving (discomfort) go away. The psychological term for this is *negative reinforcement*. Addiction is "negatively reinforced" because the uncomfortable feeling -- the craving -- goes away. The addiction is also "positively reinforced" by whatever benefits you obtain from the addiction. With this double reinforcement, it's no wonder that addictions can be difficult to change!

Like hunger, craving for your addiction occurs at times, but not all the time. It is cyclic, or periodic. Similarly, your craving has not been with you all your life. It arose after repeated experience with your addiction. If you had not had the experience, you would not have developed the craving. Although presumably everyone experiences hunger and thirst from birth (and later develops sexual craving), only individuals with specific additional experiences have those specific cravings. If your experience with a substance or activity ends, in time the related cravings go away. Eliminate the experience, and in time you eliminate the craving.

The first step in learning how to manage and ultimately eliminate craving is to monitor it. Three different aspects of craving can easily be monitored: frequency (how often it happens), intensity (how strong it is, rated on a 0 to 10 scale) and duration (how long it lasts). For instance, you might have one craving in an hour, which is a 9 on a 10 point scale (10 is strongest), and which lasts 20 minutes. Or, you could have had one craving in the last two weeks, which was a 1 on a 10 point scale, and which lasted 5 seconds.

By monitoring cravings you can confirm that cravings do not occur all the time. If it is indeed true for you that cravings do not occur all the time, then overcoming your addiction may be easier than you imagined. You will need to be dealing with cravings only when they arise, rather than dealing with them all the time.

Sometimes cravings appear to arise entirely "out of the blue," but many times they are predictable. For instance, you know from past experience that you are more likely to have cravings with certain persons, in certain places, at certain times or in certain kinds of situations. For instance, if your addiction is drinking, you are more likely to have craving in a bar than when you are not in a bar. If your addiction involves drug use, you are more likely to have a craving around individuals you have used drugs with in the past. If you are a smoker, cravings may be quite common after a meal. If you are a coffee drinker, you may feel strong cravings for coffee or a cola whenever you are experiencing pressure at work. "Chocoholics" usually feel strong cravings when they see a box of chocolates or a chocolate bar on the kitchen counter.

These persons, places, times or situations in which cravings are more likely for you are called "high risk situations." By learning how to manage these high risk situations, you can make substantial progress in overcoming your addiction. In Chapter 10 we will discuss high risk situations in more detail.

Levels of Care for Overcoming Addiction

If you seek professional treatment you will need to choose a level of care. The initial evaluation will probably result in a recommendation on this issue, but you will need to make the final decision. In general you will do best in the lowest level of care that can be effective, because that level will least interfere with the rest of your life. Levels of care range from natural recovery (possibly assisted by reading), support group attendance, brief outpatient treatment (1 or 2 visits), outpatient treatment (up to dozens of visits, typically weekly), intensive outpatient treatment (multiple visits per week for weeks to months), inpatient hospital treatment (days to weeks), and residential treatment (weeks to months). There are also variations on these levels.

For someone with basic social support there is little evidence to suggest that inpatient or residential care is better than outpatient care, although withdrawal (detoxification) may need to be managed in hospital for up to several days. I suggested in Chapter 6 that individual (outpatient) psychotherapy and couples therapy are the settings of choice for most individuals seeking treatment to overcome addiction. It also may be easier to find a psychotherapist who will provide scientifically validated treatment than to find a treatment "program" that does so. Consistent with the recommendation above to seek the lowest level of care, efforts at self-change (natural recovery), possibly guided by a workbook such as this one, are the first step. If self-change fails, higher levels of care can be accessed, all the way to the top (residential) if necessary. Traditional programs used to place patients into inpatient care even if a lower level might have been sufficient. The goal was partly to prevent "early stage addicts and alcoholics" from progressing to more severe stages. Managed care has mostly ended this practice. Chapter 10 discusses how difficult it can be to learn how to cope with craving while in inpatient care.

Although managed care has reduced the financial waste from excessive inpatient care, it has not improved some other standards of addiction care. The premise of managed care is that by providing oversight of treatment decisions treatment will both improve in quality and cost less. However, managed carriers continue to certify (traditional) addiction treatments that have not been scientifically validated. How could nonvalidated treatment be quality treatment?

Several factors apparently come together to perpetuate this problem. Decision makers about treatment in managed care firms typically adopt the traditional approach, rather than the approach supported in the scientific literature. Upper management is busy adjusting to the rapidly changing healthcare marketplace and doesn't supervise clinical decision making adequately. Employers and other purchasers of healthcare often don't know enough to ask for nontraditional treatment. I believe that this situation will change, but years -- maybe decades -- of time will be needed at the current rate of change. In the meantime, isn't it good to know that some alternative professionals, support groups, and literature are already available?

Proving You're Clean: Drug And Alcohol Testing At Home

If the government (via the legal or regulatory systems) or your employer take an interest in your substance use, you may be under some degree of coercion to provide a sample of your urine, blood, hair, saliva, sweat or breath for testing. However, if someone close to you is interested in substance testing, you may be quite willing to cooperate.

I have seen couples (or parents and children) get into severe arguments which can be summarized as one partner accusing the other of addictive behavior, and the other one denying it. The ability to have immediate evidence can prevent this argument. One partner is reassured that if there is suspicion it can be checked out, and the other is reassured that it is possible to prove innocence. Although you can go to an emergency room, doctor's office or laboratory to obtain testing, this is relatively expensive and inconvenient. In recent years inexpensive screening tests have been developed. The tests are quite accurate but not definitive. If one partner strongly disagrees with the result, laboratory testing can be done, but I haven't ever seen this second step taken. What most frequently happens is that home screening tests are obtained, both partners feel reassured, and the tests are used once or not at all. The watchful partner also may be willing to stop various attempts at monitoring or controlling the using partner once quick testing is an option, which again is a relief to both partners.

There are tests for alcohol (using breath or saliva) and other drugs (using drops of urine). Small quantities of the tests can be purchased. They have a shelf life of months to a year or more. For the purpose I have just described, a single purchase of under $20 may be sufficient.

In the case of alcohol, taking Antabuse daily and having this observed by your partner is an alternative to testing on request. Either testing or Antabuse can be effective in building trust (and supporting change), but one may be preferable according to your specific situation.

One caution: Although anyone may purchase alcohol screening tests, FDA regulations prohibit the sale of other drug screening tests directly to the public. You will need to arrange for use of other drug screening tests under the supervision of a professional.

One distributor of screening tests is

> Alco-Pro
> P.O. Box 10954
> Knoxville, TN 37939
> 800-227-9890
> FAX 800-655-5834
> 423-588-4513

Questions . . .

1. How do you experience hunger? Describe the cognitive, emotional and physical aspects of it:

2. In Project 1, Chapter 2, I suggested that you observe your cravings to determine if there were any differences for you between cravings for different substances or activities. Since you have begun this workbook, have you noticed any changes in your experience of craving?

3. What similarities and differences between hunger and your other cravings do you observe? Are they all similar enough that it makes sense to you to lump them together?

4. I suggested in Project 1, Chapter 2, that for some individuals craving is often prevented by the addiction, rather than acted upon after it occurs. This is often true for smokers or overeaters. To what extent do you think your addiction is a way to prevent craving? If craving prevention occurs frequently, how upsetting is it to you when you experience craving itself?

5. Craving can be rated on a 0 to 10 scale, with 10 being the strongest craving you have ever had. What different substances or activities have you craved, at a 5 or higher, at any point in your life?

6. What are some substances or activities that you have been significantly exposed to that you have never craved? (See the list of addictions opposite page 1 if you need suggestions.)

7. You know others who have cravings for substances or activities that you do not have cravings for. What is it like to be around them when they are craving and you are not?

8. What do you imagine it is like for others to be around you when you are craving and they are not?

9. What is it like to be around someone who is craving something you are also craving?

10. At what age did you begin having a significant craving for any substance (other than food) or activity? At what times did other cravings begin?

11. What are the substances or activities that you once craved, but no longer crave (or no longer crave to a significant degree)? You might wish to consult your answer to Question 5, Chapter 2, which asks about addictions you have overcome or reduced.

12. Have there been periods in your life when craving was usually stronger or weaker than it is now? Describe these periods:

Projects . . .

Begin monitoring your cravings for *frequency* (how often they happen), *intensity* (how strong they are, rated on a 0 to 10 scale) and *duration* (how long they last). Carry a small notebook or something similar to do this. Make three columns for each entry, as pictured below. Record the length of the craving, the peak intensity (0-10), and the situation that seemed to prompt the craving (e.g., someone yelled at me, it was after work, I was bored, etc.)

Craving record   Date:

Length (in minutes)	Peak intensity (0 to 10, with 10 being the strongest craving you ever had)	Situation (persons, places times, activities, feelings, events, "out of the blue," etc.)

Collect this information for as long as it takes to observe some patterns. What patterns do you observe?

What's Important Now?

If you date your answers to these questions, the answers over time will become a diary of your growth. It is likely that in future readings of this chapter different ideas will be important to you, reflecting the fact that you are indeed changing.

Which ideas from this chapter are most useful *to you, now?*

How can you put these ideas into action?

How much confidence do you have in your judgement in selecting these ideas as crucial at this time? (Circle a number; 10 is highest confidence)

0   1   2   3   4   5   6   7   8   9   10

Notes

9

Understanding Craving

The universe is change, our life is what our thoughts make it.
-- Marcus Aurelius (121-180 AD),
Meditations, Book 4, 3.

Overview

Cravings are time-limited. If a craving is not acted upon, it goes away. Cravings are uncomfortable, but not painful. Craving does not fundamentally interfere with your ability to make decisions. Cravings cannot force you to act on them. Craving in itself, if not acted on, is harmless. Despite the harmlessness of craving, in severe addiction we act on craving as if our survival depended on it.

The Fatigue Principle

Unless you are experiencing a craving at the moment, every craving that you have ever had has gone away. Either you engaged in the addiction (which makes the craving go away), or it went away on its own (although you might not have realized that it would). Even if you had wanted to continue the craving, it would have gone away.

Cravings, like most mental states, cannot persist for long, even if we want them to. The nervous system is in constant change. Distraction is the typical state of our awareness, not concentration. Consider meditation, which is the attempt to concentrate exclusively on something. Only with long practice can you accomplish such concentration for any significant length of time. The nervous system's constant change occurs for reasons which are not completely understood. Fortunately, we can take advantage of this constant change without fully understanding why it happens.

I call this aspect of nervous system functioning *the fatigue principle*. One might say that the nervous system just gets tired of being a certain way and moves on to being another way. Our nervous systems, like ourselves, are easily bored.

Imagine entering a room with an enduring foul smell. Although the smell persists, your awareness of it diminishes in a few minutes.

The type of behavioral psychotherapy known as exposure therapy also relies on the fatigue principle. Exposure therapy is used to overcome fears. Although the therapy can be taxing on the client, it is conceptually simple. If the client is exposed to a feared situation and stays in the situation long enough, the fear will diminish, even if the client makes no effort at all to bring about this reduction. The therapy can be done rapidly, by exposing the client continuously to the most feared situation (usually for several hours) until the fear is substantially reduced. Repeat exposures may be needed, but the bulk of the improvement usually occurs in the first exposure. As you might imagine, most clients prefer the method of gradual exposure. A list of feared situations is developed, and the client starts with the least feared situation, staying in it until the fear is substantially reduced. Then the next most feared situation is confronted, and so forth.

Perhaps the most dramatic example of the fatigue principle is the elimination of hunger by fasting. In Chapter 8 I mentioned that craving will increase until it is acted upon. The discomfort is why the craving is motivating, so the craving is often acted on. But this is only the first part of the story. If the craving is not acted on, eventually it peaks and diminishes. If you skipped breakfast and skipped lunch ,you might be quite hungry by mid-afternoon. But if you continue not eating, somewhere during the first 24 hours, for most individuals, hunger goes away. You obviously still need the food, but you no longer feel hungry. You could say that your nervous system got bored with feeling hungry, and moved on to feeling something else.

Just as your nervous system can get bored with feeling hungry, it can get bored with feeling anything. If you're impulsive and tend to act quickly on your feelings, you might not have realized this. Feelings, like craving, are time-limited. Learn to outwait them and your behavior can become much more stable.

You do not need to make a craving go away; it will go away on its own. As mentioned in Chapter 8, cravings will subside over time if you stop experiencing the substance or activity. Remembering these two facts can be of enormous help when the next craving occurs ("this one will go away, eventually they will all go away"). However, you can also hasten a craving's departure and cope well with the craving's discomfort while it lasts. We'll work on how to do this in the next chapter.

Craving Is Uncomfortable but Not Painful
Cravings are uncomfortable, but they are not truly painful. For instance, you may have experienced injuries or illnesses that caused substantial physical pain. Most individuals state that the discomfort associated with cravings is not nearly as

powerful as the pain they experienced from physical injury or illness ("the discomfort of craving and the pain from my broken leg were not even in the same universe"). This comparison helps put the discomfort of cravings in perspective. If you could manage the pain of injury and illness, how much easier would it be to manage the discomfort of cravings? Probably much easier.

There is an irony in the self-help literature about some addictions, particularly overeating. It takes effort, and tolerating some discomfort, in order to change addiction. Some approaches appear to suggest that change can occur effortlessly and entirely comfortably. We intuitively understand that this is false, and we may ironically think that the effort and discomfort are even bigger than we had imagined. If so, we may decline even beginning to change. An honest weight loss book could be titled "Eat less, do more, weigh less," but it might not sell well to individuals who have magical expectations about how change occurs.

Craving Cannot Force Action

Cravings are uncomfortable and can lead to feeling distracted and irritable, just as hunger can. However, cravings do not basically interfere with your ability to think or make decisions. Craving will not cause you to lose control of your mind. Craving can't make you do anything that you do not otherwise want to do.

An aspect of craving not yet mentioned is that it includes a range of misleading and manipulative thoughts. When craving occurs, not only do you feel a strong desire for the addiction, part of you is trying to talk you into doing it. The attempts at persuasion may include clever or even ingenious suggestions about how to engage in the addiction and "get away with it" ("If you do it this way, no one will find out," as if the fact that *you* will know doesn't count). The attempted persuasions are one-sided because they don't focus on the negative consequences if you act on the craving. Because they are one-sided they *can* be persuasive unless you are able to "step back and see the big picture." The techniques in the next chapter can be used to get an accurate perspective on the misleading statements you hear during craving.

You may have heard someone describe an "uncontrollable craving" or "uncontrollable urge." The related phrase "the devil made me do it" was once popular. Those who truly believe this are mistaken. Often, however, saying you believe it is a type of excuse or rationalization, a form of deception or manipulation. You may have told these things to yourself or others. Let's examine their accuracy.

In Chapter 7 I proposed the gun-to-the-head scenario and assumed that under those conditions everyone unless suicidal would choose to stop the addiction. Let's change the scenario a little. Instead of holding the gun to your head, I offer to give you a $100 bill for every minute you stay stopped (that's $6000 an hour or about $12 million a year). How long could you stay stopped under these circumstances? Suppose the money doesn't interest you as much, but something else does, and I offer to give it to you, perhaps a little at a time. How long could you stay stopped under these circumstances?

It would probably not take nearly so large a reward to get you stopped. A much smaller amount of money would work for most of us. There is a flip side, as well, related to costs. In daily life a minor cost is often sufficient to stop someone. For instance, a drinker may have alcoholic beverages available, but not preferred ones, so no drinking occurs. A gambler may want a game, but doesn't want to go out to find one. Earlier we used the example of a coke user who could get money by selling something, but is unwilling to do so.

Addiction prevention experts know that even modest increases in taxes on cigarettes or alcohol reduce consumption. The larger the tax, the larger the reduction. These commodities, like most commodities, are said to be "price sensitive." The tobacco and alcohol industries know this as well and vigorously oppose tax increases. They are much more supportive of media campaigns about the dangers of their products, perhaps because these campaigns don't work as well as tax increases to reduce consumption.

When you say "I couldn't stop myself" what you really mean is that you wanted to engage in your addiction, and you could not at that moment think of a strong enough reason not to. In the gun-to-the-head scenario I provided a strong enough reason, and you stopped. There are also many lesser reasons that might stop you as well, but this varies greatly from individual to individual.

As noted in Chapter 7, all individuals with addiction already exercise a degree of control, but not enough to prevent them from experiencing significant negative consequences from addiction. If you improve that degree of control sufficiently to eliminate significant negative consequences, and are still involved with the substance or activity, we call it moderation, not addiction. By thinking that you are out of control, you lose sight of the level of control you already have. Instead, identify that level of control and figure out how to build on it.

There are, of course, some things over which you have little or no control. What happens to you from the outside is often totally out of your control (e.g., you are rear-ended by another driver while at a red light). Sometimes, though, we have influence over what happens on the outside (by driving defensively we might prevent or lessen some accidents). On the other hand, some of our own behavior is basically out of our control. We die, we sneeze, we collapse from exhaustion, we get infections. Although we may have a degree of influence over the timing and severity of these events as well, clearly influence is limited.

But acting on craving is something we can have complete control over, if we choose to exercise that control. When we don't exercise it, we are in essence saying that we don't care enough to, that stopping or moderating is not important enough. We'd rather experience the benefits of addiction, and are willing to pay the costs. If the costs keep increasing, however, in time we may care. With luck we decide to change before the costs become severe or long-lasting.

Consider this issue from a different perspective. What would complete "out of control" addiction be? For a drinker it would mean ripping the top off a bottle and consuming it in one gulp, handling the next bottle identically, and continuing until loss of consciousness. Although a few teenage boys occasionally drink this way, that's about the extent of this type of drinking. Even these teenagers typically don't immediately return to this type of drinking upon regaining consciousness, although this return would be consistent with the concept of complete loss of control. The out of control smoker would chain smoke (one right after the other, as fast as possible) every waking moment. But even "chain smokers" slow down at times. The out of control gambler would gamble continuously, perhaps pausing to sleep or eat when exhausted, until every possible financial resource is used up. Although all of these scenarios are possible, they in fact happen rarely.

Learning is sometimes about entering new territory and gathering new information there. Sometimes learning is about getting a new perspective on what is right in front of you. The concept of "loss of control" has been kept in front of us for a while. What we need to realize instead is that there is always some degree of control, and where there is some control there can be greater control. You may *feel* powerless, but change begins with recognizing and building on your already-existing strengths.

Craving Is Not Dangerous

Besides fearing the discomfort of craving, some individuals fear that the state of craving itself is somehow dangerous or harmful. Perhaps if I experience a craving long enough, I will go crazy, or run screaming from where I am, or do something really embarrassing?

In Chapter 7 I noted that the best predictor of the future is the past. How much damage has a craving actually done to you? By comparison, how much damage have you feared?

The danger of craving is that it increases the possibility of engaging in your addiction. If you don't act on the craving, the worst the craving can do is distract you somewhat for a while. If you stay focused on irrational thoughts about craving, such as "this could make me crazy," you, of course, could get pretty upset. But this upset isn't caused by the craving; its caused by how you react to the irrational thoughts. With luck, you now know enough to combat this irrational thought.

Addiction as Survival: "I can't live without it"

There is a striking set of facts about the tenacity of severe addiction. Many individuals with severe addiction seem to understand that the cost-benefit analysis of their addiction reveals that the costs far outweigh the benefits. They may even say that they no longer enjoy the addiction. Nevertheless, they continue, and they state that they are compelled to do it, or words to that effect. Of course, they do have a degree of control, but they don't recognize how much they have. Even though they recognize the senselessness and self-destructiveness of the addiction, their fear of not being able to connect with the substance or activity is intense. The intensity of this fear is reminiscent of the fear someone might have if survival were at stake.

In addiction craving over time becomes a signal that elicits a survival response. When you see a bear in the woods, you mobilize to survive. When the severely addicted individual has a craving, a similar response seems to be mobilized. Over time craving has become, to a greater and greater degree, a signal that survival is at stake. Let's look at how this could occur.

All living organisms are oriented to survive. Craving, in its various forms, is part of what helps us survive. Because of craving we are negatively reinforced, even as infants, for eating and for drinking fluids. Therefore, we are likely to eat and drink regularly. In addiction the basic cravings of hunger and thirst and sex are joined by cravings for one or more addictions. The addictive cravings are then supported by brain systems with the same intensity that the basic cravings are.

In order for addictive cravings to become linked with basic cravings several steps need to occur. You need to have engaged in an addiction for some time, and the addiction needs to do something so useful for you that it can be viewed, at least by some system of your brain, as enhancing survival. Science is quite far from understanding the brain physiology involved, and a good understanding of it may lead to revisions of the simple view I am presenting here. However, let's consider the evidence supporting this conception of addictive craving as becoming akin to basic cravings like hunger and thirst.

First, one more piece of background information about how your brain works. Although it is tempting to think of the human brain as a harmoniously integrated learning and experiencing machine, the reality is that in many ways the brain is a set of autonomously functioning systems that don't always coordinate or communicate well with one another. Consider these examples:

> *You cut your finger. It hurts. You wash and bandage it, and otherwise do everything you can consciously do to repair the damage and prevent further damage. Even though there is nothing left for you to be motivated to do for your finger, the pain persists. Why? The system in your brain that generates*

the pain is unaffected by the efforts you have made for your finger. In a well-integrated system, shouldn't the pain stop after the bandage goes on?

On a Sunday night you decide to begin a diet the next day. You calculate a daily calorie budget which has more than enough calories for survival, but few enough to allow you to lose weight. This budget, or course, also has fewer calories than you have been used to eating. As you finish your dinner on Monday, with its reduced but adequate portion, you still feel hungry. In a well-integrated system, wouldn't the hunger stop when you finish dinner?

Close your eyes, and picture the home you grew up in, or some other well-known place. Look it over, and picture yourself moving around the outside and inside. Now retrace your steps, but also observe your eyes. Most of us will have our eyes move as if we were actually seeing what is in the image. Our eyes are actually seeing the backs of our eyelids, but they are scanning and accommodating as if they were in the image. In a well-integrated system, would your eyes move?

Perhaps you can recall once thinking that something was dangerous, and then realizing that it wasn't. If you have been fearful of it for a while, the fear will not go away just because your understanding has changed. Many phobics recognize, outside of the phobic situation, that their fears are irrational. Inside the situation this recognition is greatly reduced. Inside the situation they act as though their survival depends on escape. In a well-integrated system, wouldn't fear always be proportional to danger as we rationally understood it?

You may recall Pavlov's famous experiments with dogs. A tube to measure salivation was surgically inserted. A bell was rung, and food presented quickly thereafter. After several pairings of bell and food the dog begins salivating at the sound of the bell. Before the pairings the food would elicit salivation, but not the bell. After the pairings both elicit salivation. Imagine a human being in the same experiment. Now imagine telling the individual that the experiment is over and that the bell ringing will no longer mean that food is coming. Then the bell rings. The individual salivates!

You may have noted that throughout this workbook I have suggested that you use your imagination. Imagination is one way that you can make the lack of integration of your brain work for you. An imaginary experience can be almost as good as a real experience. Imaginary practice of a skill, for instance, can improve the skill even when actual practice is not available. If you are a pianist but not able to sit at your piano (perhaps because you are travelling), isn't it good to know that imaginary practice can be helpful?

Apparently after repeated experience with an addiction, one or more systems of the brain judge the effects of addiction to be crucial to survival. When the craving occurs, it is therefore not just an urge to have pleasure or to cope with a problem. Craving is now also interpreted, at least by that brain system, as being a signal that survival is at stake. That system then signals other systems, eliciting their efforts to promote survival. The systems just signalled do not attempt to interpret the message they have received. They just act on it, like a computer: "garbage in, garbage out."

If you are slow to act on the craving, or don't act on it at all, the brain system that interprets craving as a survival signal thinks you are going to die. Because of the relatively autonomous functioning of brain systems, the systems that understand that you are *not* going to die are not necessarily able to override the system sending the panic signals or the systems mobilizing survival efforts.

This idea of autonomous brain systems may also help explain the "automatic behavior" that many report when they are attempting to change. If a brain system has decided to engage in the addiction, regardless of what other systems might think of this action, it may just go ahead and do it. Other brain systems become aware of the behavior later and wonder what happened: "There I was, three bites into a piece of cheesecake from the refrigerator, but the last thing I remember thinking before that was something about work when I was in the living room a minute before. I did the whole thing on auto-pilot: get a plate, a knife and a fork, cut a piece, and eat three bites!" As addiction is more severe, this automatic behavior is more common.

No wonder addictions can be difficult to change! All this could make it sound impossible to change. However, just as in phobias and other behavioral problems, it is possible for higher brain systems to override lower ones, if sufficient time is taken and appropriate methods are used. Some form of behavioral training is required. In the case of irrational fears, we have already mentioned exposure therapy. If someone can be persuaded to stay in the feared situation long enough, the fatigue principle sets in, and the fear subsides. If seeing is believing, the part of the brain generating the irrational fear can now "observe" that death has not occurred. After a few exposures this brain part no longer generates a strong survival signal in that situation.

The way to overcome craving is also exposure training, and it is covered in the next chapter. Fortunately the "I can't live without it" scenario is relative to the extent of addictive experience. Most individuals with mild to moderate levels of addictive experience, and many with severe levels, can conduct their own exposure training, without needing professional assistance. However the exposure occurs, it leads us to act in a consistent manner, rather than having different brain systems hijack our behavior for periods of time. From this perspective, to act consistently, to act as one person instead of many, is a hallmark of behavioral health. I believe this consistency is part of what Socrates meant when he said "know thyself."

I have suggested a plausible explanation covering some aspects of why addiction might be difficult to change, and I have anchored that explanation in readily observable facts about brain functioning. Other explanations of addiction's persistence have been anchored in data about brain functioning also. I want to point out a potential misinterpretation of some of the recent scientific findings about the effects of substances on the brain. This misinterpretation can make change seem impossible.

You may have seen scans of brains that were "high on drugs" and heard the commentary that some drugs seem to "take over" the pleasure center of the brain, thereby reducing the pleasure one can experience from nondrug sources. These descriptions provide one way of explaining why someone might continue with a substance addiction. However, they fail to identify what is more important, which is how to overcome an addiction.

The misinterpretation here is that the "taking over the pleasure center" scenario is a *complete* explanation of what is occurring. If certain drugs can take over the pleasure center, then no one would stop using them. But many if not most individuals, even the severely addicted, stop altogether or moderate significantly. Therefore, something else besides "taking over the pleasure center" must also be occurring. Otherwise, changing addiction wouldn't happen. But it does, and the next chapter will show you some crucial steps in the process.

Questions . . .

1. If you did the Project in the previous chapter, you may already have some information about how your cravings are time-limited. However, the Project did not address how your cravings ended. Review that Project now. Are there any patterns to how your cravings ended? To what extent did craving just go away without any effort on your part?

2. What significant physical pains have you experienced in life? How do these pains compare to the discomfort of a craving?

3. If you are a woman, and have delivered a child, and did not mention this experience in the Question above, how would you compare the discomfort of cravings with the sensations of childbirth?

4. What's more important to you than your addiction? What would you *not* be willing to experience or have happen for the sake of your addiction (e.g., whose head could I hold a gun to, to get you to stop)? Can you think of less extreme examples?

5. This chapter has suggested that you have a degree of control over your addiction, and that it would be important to recognize that control and build on it. Question 4 is one approach to identifying the degree of control you already have. Perhaps you can identify other aspects of your self-control (e.g., the persons, places, times, situations that reduce your addictive involvement or eliminate it)? How could you start to build upon what you already have?

6. To what extent have you thought that "craving makes me do this?" What do you think of this idea now?

7. Has it ever seemed that craving was taking control of your mind, and forcing you to think about things you did not want to think about? What do you think of this idea now?

8. In what ways have you thought that the experience of craving itself might be dangerous?

9. To what extent does it seem that your mind is a collection of loosely coordinated but independently operating parts? What personal experiences might fit this description?

10. To what extent does engaging in your addiction seem necessary in order to survive? When not acting on cravings, to what extent do you have a sense of impending doom?

11. Although one or more systems of your brain may think that without your addiction you will die, what do you think of this idea? How dangerous would it be for you to be without your addiction for an extended period of time? How would your life be during this time?

12. To what extent have you used exposure to feared situations or objects as a method to overcome one or more fears?

Projects . . .

1. If you have never fasted yourself, ask among your acquaintances to discover those who have. According to these individuals, does their hunger go away when fasting? How long does it take?

2. Early in this chapter we noted that concentration is the exception in mental life, distraction the norm. Meditation was given as an example of the effort required to achieve concentration. If you have past experience with meditation, or an inclination to learn it now, try one or more periods of meditation. One form of meditation to try is to follow your breathing, without controlling it. When we are aware of our breathing, we can control it, but most of the time it happens without our awareness. In this meditation you are aware of breathing but attempting not to control it. What effect does meditating have on your sense of well-being? What effect does meditating have on your ability to recall the conclusions of your cost-benefit analysis?

3. The next time you have a very strong feeling, observe it carefully. If possible, don't act on it immediately. What happens?

What's Important Now?

If you date your answers to these questions, the answers over time will become a diary of your growth. It is likely that in future readings of this chapter different ideas will be important to you, reflecting the fact that you are indeed changing.

Which ideas from this chapter are most useful *to you, now*?

How can you put these ideas into action?

How much confidence do you have in your judgement in selecting these ideas as crucial at this time? (Circle a number; 10 is highest confidence)

0   1   2   3   4   5   6   7   8   9   10

10

Coping With Craving

I couldn't help it. I can resist everything except temptation
-- Oscar Wilde (1854-1900)
Lady Windermere's Fan, Act I, 1893

Overview

Cravings are normal for you and will continue during the first weeks to months of abstinence. They may last even longer if you are moderating. You are not responsible for the existence of craving, only for your response to it. You can cope with craving by avoiding high risk situations, substituting other substances or activities, redirecting your attention, counterarguing it, or by distracting yourself. During your initial efforts at change it may be better to use avoidance and substitution. As you gain confidence reduce avoidance and substitution, and bring out cravings regularly so that you stay in practice for dealing with them. When cravings occur spontaneously, consider them as a sign that some problem needs to be identified and solved, and as a reminder of the progress you have made. Refusing offers from others to engage in the addiction is not difficult if you are prepared.

Cravings Are Normal For You, For Now

Craving apparently arises from one of the brain systems that cannot immediately be controlled by a decision. You can decide to stop (or moderate) today, but cravings will last weeks to months more. Craving for moderators may last even longer, but the degree of addiction is also a factor. As I mentioned in Chapter 7, moderators tend to be individuals with mild to moderate problems, not severe ones. The more severe your addiction, the longer your cravings are likely to last after changing. Smokers are over-represented among those with long-lasting cravings, perhaps because smoking is repeated so often each day.

For most individuals cravings are gone or virtually gone within a year. Even if cravings do not entirely disappear after successful change, they are dramatically fewer, weaker and shorter. If you had headaches that occurred every day, lasted for hours at a time, were 9s and 10s on a 10 point scale, and then as a result of relaxation training you had headaches that occurred once a month, for a half hour, and were 1s or 2s, wouldn't you consider this a major success?

Craving arises in a brain system for which actions speak louder than words. The decision to change is meaningless to it. It is changing that counts. To complicate matters, when you first change, craving may get worse for a while, perhaps the first week or two. This increase often occurs and does not mean that you have a lack of motivation.

Craving will diminish over time, but you may also experience a sudden flare-up, even months later. Usually these flare-ups, in retrospect, are explainable. For instance, you might get visited by an former "addiction buddy." If your progress has been good until that point, it might not even occur to you that the buddy's presence will have an effect on you. I think of these flare-ups as a good sign, a last gasp. In World War II, on December 16, 1944, the German army initiated the "Battle of the Bulge," which created a bulge in the Allied front in Western Europe. The German army was unable to sustain the effort, and on January 8, 1945, the bulge began collapsing. Germany surrendered May 8, 1945. If you experience a battle of the bulge (my apologies to the overeaters), adopt a long-term perspective on it!

Craving Happens, But You Choose Your Response

The occurrence of craving itself is beyond your control. There is no single act that can with certainty eradicate all future craving. There are steps that can influence its occurrence (we will discuss them shortly), but ultimately craving will show up when it shows up. What you do have full control over is what to do about craving. To reiterate a crucial point, if you think of a strong enough reason not to act on the craving, then you won't, and in time that craving and all craving will go away.

Ways to Cope With Craving

You can cope with craving by avoiding high-risk situations, substituting another substance or activity, redirecting your attention, counterarguing it, or distracting yourself. We will consider each of these methods in turn. Often craving coping involves elements of more than one method. If I label a technique as primarily involving distraction, and you think of it as primarily counterarguing, this is not a problem. It's the process, and not the labels, that matters. If you are familiar with techniques for coping with anxiety, you may recognize these craving coping techniques as similar.

◆ **Aversive Conditioning.** Before describing techniques you can apply yourself, let's consider one professional technique, aversive conditioning. In aversive conditioning the nervous system is trained to associate your addiction with some highly unpleasant (painful) experience. The training occurs by pairing together the addiction and the experience several times. In exposure therapy we attempt to un-pair fear and some situation. In aversive conditioning we do the opposite, pairing unpleasantness and some situation, so that the situation will be feared and avoided in the future.

Sometimes aversive pairings happen naturally. One addict I know was sitting in his dealer's home when the police (unexpectedly!) stormed it. The dealer began raising a gun to his head and said "You snitched on me, I'm going to kill you." The police stopped the dealer just before the trigger was pulled.

An experimental psychologist might describe this occurrence as *one-trial learning*. This individual did not experience another craving from that moment until at least a year later (when I first heard the story). Unfortunately, like the earlier gun-to-the-head scenario, this sort of treatment is difficult to arrange!

Professionals can apply aversive conditioning in several ways. The addiction can be paired with a drug that will make you vomit, with electrical shock, or with any highly unpleasant actual experience or a highly unpleasant imaginary experience. After several pairings craving is gone. Booster sessions later usually will be needed to maintain the effect, but the respite from craving can be dramatic. During this respite the remainder of one's life can be improved so that when craving does return coping with it will be much easier. If you are intensely afraid of craving, this technique may be for you.

A behavior therapist who does aversive conditioning can work with you to pair an unpleasant imaginary experience with imagined addictive experience. Shick Shadel Hospital (800-272-8464) in Seattle, Washington, has since 1935 employed, among other techniques, aversive conditioning using nausea inducing medications and electrical shock. Although it is possible to apply aversive conditioning to yourself, if you are motivated enough to persist in applying the unpleasant stimulation of the conditioning, you are probably adequately motivated to benefit from the techniques listed below.

◆ **Avoid high-risk situations.** We discussed in Chapter 7 how changes of circumstance could have a significant effect on your ability to change an addiction. Many situations may trigger a craving, but a few trigger it so consistently and strongly as to be considered high-risk situations. High-risk situations are also situations in which you typically engage in your addiction, even if you are not aware of significant cravings there. You may become involved in your addiction so quickly in these situations that there is little time for the craving to develop.

In the early stages of learning to cope with cravings your confidence may be low. For instance, you may be confident that you can cope with cravings up to a 3 on a 10-point scale, but uncertain about 4s to 7s, and somewhat confident that you *would* slip if you experienced 8s to 10s. Rather than take the risk of slipping, it is often easiest to avoid some situations entirely.

Consider the following overlapping categories of high-risk situations, and some examples of each. In the *Questions* you will be asked again about high-risk situations, but for now, consider which ones apply to you:

⇒ *individuals* (partners, friends, roommates, dealers, coworkers)

⇒ *groups* (softball team, poker buddies, my family, the guys on the corner)

⇒ *times* (before or after or during: meals, work, weekends, holidays, happy hour, stressful days)

⇒ *places* (work, bars, your car, friends' places, dealers' places, casinos, card rooms, the living room, the kitchen, the bedroom, the garage, the back yard or porch, the street corner, pool rooms)

⇒ *activities/situations* (holidays, celebrations, parties, traveling, concerts, reunions, get-togethers, business meetings)

⇒ *other specific addiction cues* (social pressure to engage in the addiction, bad feelings, conflict with others, feeling good and wanting to feel better, specific songs, sight or smell of the substance or activity, paraphernalia associated with the substance or activity)

Your addiction may occur in relatively few situations. If your addiction is severe (meaning much of your life is organized around it), it may occur at almost any time or place. Your addiction is happening so regularly that instead of situations influencing the addiction, the addiction is largely controlling the situations you are in. Regardless of how severe your addiction is, more than avoidance may be required to overcome it, but avoidance is often a good place to begin coping with craving. If it is not realistic to avoid a high-risk situation (e.g., you have an internet addiction but you need to use your computer at work), other methods for coping with these situations will be needed. On the other hand, you may not need to go to some of these situations again, as they may no longer fit into the life you are building for yourself.

You may have paraphernalia or substances or other reminders of your addiction that could be thrown away. For some individuals keeping them around is a source of pride, and for others a continuous source of craving. You will need to decide how much to get rid of. A related issue is whether those you live with engage in the same addiction. You might ask them not to expose you to the addiction, or to overcome the addiction also. You might decide that it is better to move, temporarily or permanently.

If you are focused on overcoming alcohol problems, you may wish to use Antabuse. On Antabuse every situation becomes a low-risk situation (and craving may virtually disappear also). Unless you stay on Antabuse for life, however, you will eventually need other coping strategies also, but by then you will with luck be able to use them effectively. Perhaps in the future medications similar to Antabuse will be developed for other addictions.

"Advanced avoidance" involves being in a high-risk situation but having some factor (often a person) present which results in confidence that craving will not be acted on. For instance, if you need to go to an office party where drugs and alcohol will be in use, taking your spouse along may protect you. This advanced avoidance experience can be a good transition to the techniques listed below.

◆ **Substitute.** Instead of engaging in your addiction, you can use another substance (even if you have an activity addiction) or engage in some other activity (even if you have a substance addiction). Like avoidance, this is a technique to be used only at the beginning, as your confidence is building. There are a wide variety of options, so I will list only a few examples:
⇒ Drink a nonalcoholic beverage
⇒ Eat carrots or some low fat food
⇒ Go for a walk
⇒ Call a friend
⇒ Go to a support group meeting
⇒ Work
⇒ Clean house
⇒ Read a book or magazine
⇒ Go to sleep
⇒ Exercise

You can also use a substitute that is a step in the right direction, but not complete success. For instance, you could smoke pot instead of using coke, or drink instead of using heroin. Such substitutions can be helpful in the short term, but they may also lead to new addictions! The principle of "harm reduction" applies here. Any movement in the right direction (less negative consequences) is desirable, but movement is not the same as complete success.

The problem with substitution is that it keeps an equation alive: craving = do something to make it go away. If how you make it go away is less damaging than the addiction, you have reduced your harm, but you have not overcome your addiction. Similarly, if you avoid certain situations, you are living in fear of craving. In order to overcome addiction you need techniques for experiencing but not acting on craving until it dies away. Therefore, as soon as you feel you are able, go beyond avoidance and substitution to more advanced techniques.

One of the problems with traditional treatment programs is that they tend to encourage avoidance and substitution as long-term coping strategies. They may suggest that you are somehow not strong enough to cope directly with craving (because you are powerless). Although it is true you may be better off to work up to it gradually, if you do not eventually deal with cravings, you will live in fear of them or engage in substitute addictions. Attending daily support group meetings for months or years after initiating change can be an example of a substitute addiction.

One of the additional problems with traditional inpatient or residential care is that it removes you from your regular environment. You are unlikely to experience craving if the usual cues and triggers are not around you. If you don't learn how to cope in your regular environment, however, you may well relapse shortly after discharge (a not uncommon occurrence). It would be better to expose yourself to cues and triggers almost from the moment you are admitted, as well as to teach yourself the skills listed below. Then upon discharge you can have confidence, not a return to fear.

Some individuals at the beginning of a change plan stop having craving altogether. They don't seem to need even the basic strategies of avoidance and substitution. This is likely to be a short-lived situation. Cravings occur later, and the individual has not practiced coping with them. If you have no cravings at first, I strongly suggest that you immediately "bring out craving," as noted in Advanced Coping with Craving towards the end of this chapter. In this way you can be preventing a "buildup" of craving, and you are practicing the skills you will almost certainly need in the days or weeks ahead.

◆ **Redirect attention.** Redirecting attention is probably most useful when craving is small, perhaps 1 to 3 in intensity. A craving that starts out stronger will diminish as the counterarguing and distracting techniques below are used. Once the craving gets down to the 1 to 3 range, you can finish it off with redirected attention. Redirecting involves shifting attention away from acting on the craving, or outlasting the craving.

Just keep moving. The simplest response to craving is to accept it as one more element in your ever-changing stream of consciousness, and then move on. If you meditate, this is how you respond to the intrusions to your meditative state. Experienced meditators probably have fewer addiction problems. "Oh, there is another thought about doing it. But I'm going to get back to my work." For low level cravings, which may seem more like passing thoughts than a full-body craving experience, this can be an adequate response.

Study the craving. For slightly stronger cravings you might redirect your attention from the possibility of acting on the craving, to observing the craving itself. Observe it as if it is something to be studied or discussed with others. Notice how strong it is, how it seems to change in strength up or down, what seems to have brought it on (if anything), and how other thoughts and feelings in time begin to crowd it out of your mind. Talk out loud to yourself (if you are alone!) if you think this would be helpful: "I can feel a craving coming on. It is about a 3 [out of 10] now. I am also having a memory about the last time I did that and how much fun it was. That seems to make the craving move closer to a 4. But I am now also remembering the trouble I got in later, and that is bringing it down closer to a 1." At a certain point the craving may be lower, and you can use the previous technique of redirecting your attention back to what you were previously doing.

Set a timer. This technique might also be considered a distraction technique, except that active distraction is not used. Unlike the two previous redirected attention techniques, setting a timer can be used for craving of any strength. This technique works particularly well for food cravings, because kitchens are where both the food and the timers are.

Set a timer for the amount of time you are very confident you won't act on the craving. For instance, if you are confident that you can withstand the experience of the craving, however you do it, for at least 3 minutes, then set a timer for 3 minutes. While the timer is on, begin doing other activities. When the timer goes off, there is a good chance that the craving will be weaker, and less of a problem. At that point you can re-set the timer, use another technique, or act on the craving.

As you get experience with this technique, you can set the timer for longer and longer periods. At some point, the timer may be set for 20 or 30 minutes. When it goes off, you may have become so involved with something else that your first reaction might be "why was the timer on?" That craving is gone! At first, however, it is better to underestimate how long to set the timer, and reset it if necessary. If you start with 3 minutes, you can gradually increase your time as your confidence increases.

Ways to Cope with Craving

Aversive conditioning (a professional method)

Avoid and substitute (initial steps)

Redirect attention
  Just keep moving
  Study the craving
  Set a timer
  Delay beginning

Counterargue
  Recall your "benefits of changing" list (short or long)
  Complete the image of an addiction experience (don't just stop after the good
    part)
  Recall a "moment of clarity," when it was very clear change was needed
  Recall a memorized list of coping statements
  See a "benefits movie"
  Use imagery of fighting back (personify the craving)
  Imagine the backwards substance or backwards activity

Distract yourself
  Do any simple activity at high speed
  Count something
  Subtract continuously
  Say the alphabet backwards
  Read words backwards
  Look for the alphabet in order
  Tighten your muscles in a repetitive sequence
  Identify coins or other objects by feel
  Advanced distraction: focus intensely on perceptual experience (meditation)

Advanced coping with craving
  No more avoidance or substitution
  Bring out craving
  View the craving as an opportunity to identify a problem
  View the craving as a reminder you are getting your benefits
  Transform the feelings associated with craving

Be prepared to refuse offers

Ineffective coping
  Attempting to drive the craving away

Delay beginning. A variation of the previous technique is to delay the beginning of your addictive involvement, especially if you have a regular starting time. This technique is useful for increasing your capacity for coping with craving, without having you stop acting on them altogether. For instance, if you go to gamble every Saturday morning, you might go later and later, until eventually you did not go until Sunday, or did not go for the entire weekend. Once you can delay long enough, craving will die away.

◆ **Counterargue.** When craving is in the middle ranges (perhaps from 4 to 8), arguing back with it may be helpful. At this level the craving may be seductive enough that just turning away from it may not work (i.e., your attention may keep coming back to it). As mentioned in Chapter 7, when you are experiencing craving, the benefits of addiction are foremost on your mind. You have a kind of "tunnel vision," and you don't have ready mental access to the costs of addiction. If you make a decision about the craving based on just the information the craving is showing you, you will be missing some significant information!

Counterarguing can also involve recalling the benefits of overcoming addiction, or attacking the craving itself. Below are some examples of each of these themes.

Recall your "benefits of changing" list (short or long). In Chapters 3 through 5 you attempted to identify your reasons for wanting to change by doing a cost-benefit analysis. A review of these reasons is as basic a response as you can make to the presence of craving. These reasons can be summarized as the "costs of addiction," or the "benefits of stopping," or the "benefits of moderating," or in any other way meaningful to you. I suggest you make a list of up to 5 major reasons (the short list), write them down, carry them with you, and review them regularly until they are memorized. For instance, your short list (a benefits-of-stopping version) might be:

If I stop I will:
 * *have better health*
 * *be a better partner*
 * *have more self-respect*
 * *get out of debt*
 * *avoid legal problems*

When this "benefits of stopping" list is in your awareness along with the benefits of the addiction, it's easier to choose to change. In the Questions at the end of this chapter you can construct such a list for yourself. There you can also construct the long list, which you may prefer.

Complete the image of an addiction experience (don't just stop after the good part). Craving activates pleasant memories of addiction, not unpleasant ones. Typically the pleasant aspects occur early in the experience, and the unpleasant ones later. First the high, then the hangover. Buy now, pay later. As we said in Chapter 5 ("perfect addiction"), if you just got the high, and not the hangover, you would have no reason to change. But now you get both (substitute whatever terms are appropriate for your addiction).

This technique begins after craving has reminded you of the early pleasant part of the addictive experience. You keep the memory going, and visualize it all the way through to its painful ending. Again, if the ending weren't painful, you wouldn't need to be changing your addiction. As with the benefits list, when the good and bad aspects of your addiction are both in view, it's easier to choose to change.

Recall a "moment of clarity," when it was very clear change was needed. Moments of clarity are the very painful episodes that can occur because of addiction. A moment of clarity could be an arrest, a health crisis, a near-death experience, an injury, a physician's warning, the angry departure of a loved one, the loss of a home, a highly embarrassing situation, or any other serious or catastrophic event. Having one of these episodes and then making light of it, or blaming it on someone else, or blaming it on a misguided legal system, or using some other rationalization to misinterpret what happened, means that you have not had a moment of clarity. Instead, you just had one more negative consequence. A few more may be needed to persuade you.

The phrase "hitting bottom" has been used to describe how you know when you have experienced a moment of clarity. These moments can be very different for different individuals. Some individuals definitely seem to be slow learners, at least in the area of addiction. With luck you won't need to have any more moments of clarity, and you won't need to suffer any more negatives from addiction.

When craving occurs, guide your attention to memories of a moment of clarity. Remember how painful it was and how firmly you resolved to be different. Keep these memories in mind until the craving subsides.

Recall a memorized list of coping statements. In addition to reminding yourself about negative consequences, you could also remind yourself about craving:

"This craving will go away in a while if I don't act on it. If I do act on it, it will return shortly and probably be even stronger than this one. If I don't act on it *this* craving will go away, and eventually all of them will go away or become so small as not to be a bother. The craving itself won't hurt me. It's normal to have craving for now, because I just began changing. In time they will be gone. This craving can't force me to do anything, I'm the one in control."

Carry a written reminder, which includes one or more of the statements above, and pull it out when craving occurs.

See a "benefits movie." If you are a highly visual individual, you might enjoy translating your benefits list into a "movie." Suppose one of your benefits of change is having more money. Pretend that you are a movie director and "shoot" in your mind's eye a sequence of shots depicting this benefit. Tracking shot: you walking toward ATM. Close up: you inserting card and keying in PIN. Tight close up: a good sized number, your balance, showing in the screen. Tight close up: money being discharged. Tracking shot: you walking away with money in hand and a smile on your face. Such a movie can be played in your mind very quickly. It reminds you indirectly of negative consequences and directly of where you have decided you want to be going in your life. Sometimes a single picture will be sufficient, if there is one image that is especially meaningful to you (e.g., your child smiling).

Use imagery of fighting back (personify the craving). You can imagine that the craving is some type of enemy or misleading person who has now set upon you: an attacking warrior, a slick salesperson, a lying lobbyist, the devil, an animal, a monster, or any other image that has meaning to you. In imagination, fight back using means that are appropriate in your image (if it is a warrior, use similar weapons to defeat the warrior; if it is a salesperson, be assertive).

Imagine the backwards substance or backwards activity. Addictions are sometimes called *impulse disorders*. An impulse occurs only for a substance or activity that has a quick positive effect. An "impulse" for a delayed positive effect would usually be called a plan. In the case of addiction quick positive effects are followed by delayed negative effects. They come together as a package. In this technique you reverse the order. Imagine that you first get the hangover, then get the high. Imagine how appealing it would be to do it in this order. It's the same deal, only the order is reversed! Pay now, receive later. What are the chances you would engage in your addiction if it happened in this order?

◆ **Distract Yourself.** If a craving seems particularly strong, a distraction technique may be helpful. A distraction technique is any simple activity conducted at high speed. This technique is actually a variation of redirecting attention, but instead of going back to what you were doing, you focus on something that, because it is done quickly but is simple to do, captures and holds your attention. Your attention is shifted from inside to outside, from thoughts and images to perceptions. You could also consider this a concentration exercise, because you are deliberately shifting your focus (but to something that is easy to stay focused on).

For instance, look around you. Is there something in the room that you could count? It might be ceiling tiles, floor tiles, designs on wallpaper or paneling, window blinds, leaves of a plant, or something that you can observe through a window outside the room. Count the objects that you see as rapidly as you can. For instance, count the number of blinds that you see on a window. If you count very rapidly and as accurately as you can, you will find that other thoughts that were on your mind go away, because you are focused on the counting. This is one way to clear craving out of your mind.

Other simple techniques include:

⇒ *subtract numbers* (for instance, subtract 7 from 1,000 and get 993, subtract 7 again and get 986, subtract 7 again, and so on),

⇒ *say the alphabet backwards*

⇒ *read words backwards* (say the word correctly but read the sequence backwards: "backwards words read")

⇒ *play the "alphabet game"* by looking at license plates, book titles or a printed page and find an A, then a B, then a C, etc.

⇒ *tighten the muscles in your body* in a particular sequence, over and over (tighten your feet, then your calves, then your thighs, then your pelvis, then your stomach, then your chest, then your shoulders, then your neck, then your face, over and over again)

⇒ *reach into your pocket or purse* and attempt to identify coins or other objects there just by feel

Advanced Distraction. Focus on your perceptual experience fully (notice what you are seeing, hearing, touching, experiencing inside your body, smelling or tasting, either separately or in combination; possibly give a commentary about it to an imaginary listener). In its most advanced form, a distraction technique is a concentration technique, a form of meditation. If you do these kinds of activities for several minutes you will notice that the craving is mostly or entirely gone from your mind, because you have not been paying attention to it. If there is still some craving, it is probably weaker, and you could then use one of the other techniques.

◆ **Advanced Coping with Craving.** In time craving will become less commanding and frightening, if you have practiced dealing with it by not avoiding situations in which it arises or substituting other substances or activities when it occurs. Once you are confident about dealing with craving, its occurrence then presents some opportunities for you. Here are some ways to take advantage of those opportunities.

Bring out craving. Craving is partly predictable. If you imagine a pleasant addictive experience, you are more likely to experience a craving than if you are thinking about something else. You could therefore probably bring out a craving by using your imagination. There are three opportunities here. You can experience a fuller sense of self control ("I control what I focus my thoughts on, so I can have a craving or move beyond it"). You can drain away any buildup of "craving energy" that may be preparing for a "battle of the bulge." You are staying in practice for coping with craving.

As your ability to cope with craving becomes better, it may take more energetic efforts to bring out a craving. Often the opposite of avoidance is needed (e.g., not only do you walk through the casino, but you talk with an acquaintance at the slot machines). Be mindful of the risks that you may be taking in the event that you deliberately seek out high risk situations. Remember that not only bringing out the craving, but also coping with it, is part of the exercise! It would be wise to have one or more counterarguing techniques in mind, and to have practiced them in advance.

Only by coping in high-risk situations will you have full confidence that you have resolved your addiction. In my office I have paraphernalia related to various addictions. Once my client has moved beyond avoidance and substitution as primary coping techniques, I may unexpectedly place the bag of paraphernalia in the client's lap. We spend several minutes exploring the contents. There are several protective factors involved. The substances (except the alcohol) are fake. This "exposure" occurs early in the session, so that there is time for the craving to go away. I am present to help the client if difficulties arise. Although many clients are initially shocked, by the end of the session they are feeling stronger and more confident.

View the craving as an opportunity to identify and solve a problem. Think of the craving as an opportunity to recognize other problems. Typically, cravings occur in situations in which you need to cope with some kind of stress. Rather than coping directly with the stress, you get a craving. For instance, you may experience cravings in social situations, because you are nervous about being around others. Rather than acting on the craving, focus your attention on learning how to be around others. Craving can remind you of problems you need to work on.

View the craving as a reminder you are getting your benefits. Whenever you are experiencing craving, you are not actively involved in the addiction. Although you may have just been involved with it, and craving has resurfaced, as long as you are craving you are not using or acting (we don't keep wanting what we already have). Therefore, if you are craving, you are not involved and thus getting the benefits of changing. As time goes by, it is easy to begin to take these benefits for granted (we don't keep wanting what we already have). So having an occasional reminder can be helpful for keeping motivation high.

Imagine the following scenario. You have a swimming accident and go under. As you lose consciousness, your life "flashes before your eyes." Someone pulls you out and revives you before any permanent harm occurs. After this near-death experience you are extremely grateful to be alive and find a thrill even in simple pleasures, such as how green the grass is and how blue the sky is. As time goes by these thrills begin to fade for you. You begin to take life more for granted, much as you did before the drowning. But every so often some giant grabs you by the scruff of your neck, takes you to water, and holds you under until you lose consciousness again. When you revive, the grass would again be incredibly green and the sky incredibly blue.

The craving can be an uncomfortable but welcome reminder of how bad your life used to be, and how good it has become. Don't you forget it!

Transform the feelings associated with the craving. If you change your view of craving (perhaps by using one of the two techniques above), you will also transform your emotional experience of the craving. You might also try to transform the emotional experience of the craving directly, simply by suggesting to yourself a new way to feel it. For instance, instead of feeling frustrated, uncomfortable, or irritable, how about feeling energized, light, alert, clear-headed or active? There are many emotional states that can be interpreted in various ways, and what we tell ourselves about them (and the situations we find ourselves in) can have a profound impact on how we experience them. You probably don't want to experience craving as uncomfortable. Pick a new way to experience it!

◆ **Be Prepared To Refuse Offers.** There will probably be both direct and subtle (nonverbal) pressure on you at times to engage in your addiction. Your addiction companions may not like that you are changing and may try to pull you back into previous behaviors. Typically, those who do so are ambivalent about their own behavior but unwilling to face up to that ambivalence directly. It's easier not to have you as an example of someone who has changed, because that is subtle pressure on them to do something also.

These social pressures are predictable to a great degree. Social pressure is what creates many of your high-risk situations. Consequently, you probably have a good idea of the kinds of offers or subtle pressures that will occur there. You can practice in advance how you will cope with them, either in imagination or with someone you trust. Here are some general guidelines.

As already stated, *avoid these situations at first*, until ready to cope with them. If you are there at some point, practice refusal phrases in advance by saying them *out loud* a number of times (that way you can get the cracking out of your voice before you go public!). Phrases might include "No thanks, not right now; No thanks, but how about a soda? Thanks, I'll pass for now." Notice that none of the examples make a declaration like "I've quit for good." You can make a declaration if you want, but do you really? Those close to you have probably already been told. Is it important that these individuals also be told? Possibly not. You are entitled to your privacy. You risk making your decision become a focus of group discussion, with subtle and possibly direct pressure to relapse coming at you. Your companions may simply feel ill at ease with your declaration, even if they exert no pressure, and you might decide to relapse just so they (and you) will feel more comfortable again.

What if your refusal is not accepted? At first, simply *keep repeating it*, with only a little variation: "No thanks, I really don't want to right now; No thanks, but do you have any [something else]?; Really, I'll pass for now, I'll let you know later if I do want to." If this persists for several rounds, you might refocus the conversation by saying: "It is important to you that I do this, why?" Now the other person is the focus, not you. The typical response will be something about wanting to be a good host, or wanting you to have a good time, or thinking that you usually do, or something similar. Your response can be to accept the observation, and reassert that you don't want to: "You are a great host, but I still don't want to; I am having a good time, and I'd prefer to pass for now; I know I usually do, but I don't want to now." At this point changing the subject may put an end to that portion of the conversation.

Because nature abhors a vacuum, it may also be easier for you to *have some alternative activities*, while there, to engage in. The simple example is that if you are with drinkers, drink something nonlcoholic. If you choose your beverage skillfully, they may not even know its non-alcoholic. Once you have coped with this challenge several times, it will be easier, because others will begin treating you differently, and because you will be less intimidated by social pressure.

You may have noticed that coping with craving and coping with social pressure both need to be dealt with similarly. At first, avoid them. Later, practice facing them directly, until they no longer are difficult. Finally, take advantage of the opportunities they present. Experiencing social pressure is a good opportunity to remind yourself of the self-confidence and sense of identity you have developed.

◆ **An Ineffective Method.** If you attempt to drive craving out of your mind directly ("I'm not going to think about this craving"), you put yourself in a paradoxical situation. In order not to think about the craving, you need to remember what it is you're not going to think about! Thus you would be attempting to remember, but not think about, the same thing. Instead, accept the craving, then use one of the methods already mentioned.

Individuals who attempt to change addiction using this "drive craving away" method are in a precarious position. Because they don't fully experience a craving, they may not recognize that the craving will go away. They are so busy driving it away they don't discover that it leaves on its own. If you accept the discomfort of cravings in your early change process, in time cravings disappear. You are free of them, or virtually so. *You don't have to be recovering; you can be recovered.*

Questions . . .

1. If you have not begun moderating or abstaining, how long do you think significant cravings will last if you do? If you have begun, what has your experience of cravings been so far?

2. What is the single best reason you can think of to overcome your addiction? If you clearly thought of this reason each time you had a craving, what are the chances you would act on the craving? Explain your answer:

3. Consider the high risk categories listed below, and write for each your own specific high risk situations:

* *individuals* (partners, friends, roommates, dealers, coworkers)

* *groups* (softball team, poker buddies, my family, the guys on the corner)

* *times* (before or after or during: meals, work, weekends, holidays, happy hour, stressful days)

* *places* (work, bars, your car, friends' places, dealers' places, casinos, card rooms, the living room, the kitchen, the bedroom, the garage, the back yard or porch, the street corner, pool rooms)

* *activities/situations* (holidays, celebrations, parties, traveling, concerts, reunions, get-togethers, business meetings)

* *other specific addiction cues* (social pressure to engage in the addiction, bad feelings, conflict with others, feeling good and wanting to feel better, specific songs, sight or smell of the substance or activity, paraphernalia associated with the substance or activity)

4. Which of these situations would it be best for you to avoid for now? How soon might you be ready to cut back on avoidance? How fast would you expose yourself to these situations?

5. If you are ready to expose yourself to these situations, or need to for other reasons, what can you do to reduce your risk of acting on craving while there?

6. In Chapter 7 the idea of degrees of control was mentioned. You are not completely out of control of your addiction. Review again the list of situations in Question 3 above. In which ones are you unlikely to engage in your addiction? In which ones have you never engaged?

7. What risks does your current living situation present? Are there paraphernalia or substances or other reminders to consider throwing away? Do you want to request others that you live with to change any of their own behavior (recognizing that they might not change)? How helpful might moving be, temporarily or permanently?

8. What substitutions might be effective for the moment? How soon will you be ready to cut back on these substitutions?

9. In Chapters 3 through 5 you attempted to identify your reasons for wanting to change, by doing a cost-benefit analysis. Review your work in these chapters, especially the answers to Questions 6 through 10 in Chapter 4, and Questions 5 through 11 in Chapter 5. As you take a fresh look at these answers now, prepare to construct a new list. Choose one of the following titles for your list:

Benefits of Changing Addiction
Benefits of Overcoming Addiction
Benefits of Stopping (Or Abstaining)
Benefits of Moderating

First, write every significant benefit that belongs on the list (the long list). What you select will be based on the answers you gave in Chapters 4 and 5, but may also include additional insights you have had since completing those chapters. You might also wish to consult Question 12 in Chapter 5 for additional guidance on how to transform the items on the "costs of addiction" and the "benefits of addiction" checklists into one of the above lists.

(One caution: I suggest that the wording of each benefit be from an *entirely selfish* perspective. For instance, if one of the costs of addiction is impairment in your relationship, then I would word the benefit "I would be a better partner" instead of "I would please my partner." To be blunt, your addiction has been a selfish act. The motivation to overcome it needs to be equally selfish. If you initially attempt to please others, you may later wonder for whom the change is occurring. I suggest that you are unlikely to succeed unless you are clear that the change is for yourself. As we will discuss in the next chapter, as you overcome your addiction — for yourself — you will be in position to give to others — because you want to.)

Benefits List:

Having completed the long list, circle up to five of the most significant benefits (the short list). As you look at the long list and the short list, how motivated do you feel to overcome your addiction?

10. What are your moments of clarity?

11. What memorized statements might best help you cope with craving?

12. Which benefit of changing addiction might be most persuasive if you saw it as a "movie"?

13. What way of imagining a craving as a person or "being" might fit best for you? How would you fight back against this person or being?

14. If you imagined the backwards substance or backwards activity, how far back in time would you need to go to include the whole experience? (E.g., if you engage in the addiction on Saturday, when would problems begin and when would they end?)

15. Of the distraction techniques mentioned, which one seemed most suitable for you?

16. What memories or imaginary experiences could you use to bring out a craving?

17. How easy is it to think of craving as a useful reminder to face up to your problems?

18. What social pressures to engage in your addiction are you likely to face? How could you respond to them?

19. What alternative activities could you use in your most significant high risk situations?

20. Would you prefer to be recovering or recovered from your addiction?

Projects . . .

1. Pick at least one of the ways to cope with craving, study it carefully, and put it into use this week. Even if you are not fully successful in not acting on the craving, how much help does the technique provide?

2. If you are ready, write out your plans for overcoming addiction. If you are ready, put these plans into effect. What do you learn from acting on these plans?

What's Important Now?

If you date your answers to these questions, the answers over time will become a diary of your growth. It is likely that in future readings of this chapter different ideas will be important to you, reflecting the fact that you are indeed changing.

Which ideas from this chapter are most useful *to you, now*?

How can you put these ideas into action?

How much confidence do you have in your judgement in selecting these ideas as crucial at this time? (Circle a number; 10 is highest confidence)

0   1   2   3   4   5   6   7   8   9   10

Medications and Overcoming Addiction

Regardless of whether you are ready to begin overcoming your addiction, you probably want to know about all of your "action stage" options. In addition to learning about how to cope with craving, one of the prominent options is the use of prescription medications. Medication options are extensive and will not be covered comprehensively here. Medications are primarily a medical matter and not directly related to the psychological approach for overcoming addiction presented in this workbook. There is no medication that will cure your (psychological) addiction, but some may provide significant assistance.

If you have been a heavy and regular substance user, you may experience "withdrawal" if you stop the substance suddenly. Withdrawal occurs because, in addition to a psychological addiction, your body has developed a physical dependence on the substance (as mentioned in Chapter 2 these often go together but not necessarily). Your body, if physically dependent, has adapted to the presence of the substance. If the substance is abruptly withdrawn, your body adapts back again, but not without a struggle. The substances to be most concerned about are alcohol, the opiates, and various prescription medications such as barbiturates, benzodiazepines and other sedatives, hypnotics or tranquilizers. If you have used _any_ substances, a physical exam by an addiction specialist may be worth having, even if you are not concerned about withdrawal. Ideally, you will see a physician who is certified by the American Society of Addiction Medicine, but any competent physician with addiction experience is suitable. Your pharmacist is also a good source for general information on these issues (and often understands medications and their interactions better than physicians do).

Various medications can help reduce withdrawal discomfort. If withdrawal is severe, medical treatment may be necessary to save your life. Severe withdrawal is more common if you are in your 50s or older, have used many years, or have other medical problems, but it is not limited to these conditions. If you have any doubts about withdrawal, seek medical help! If necessary, go to any emergency room or urgent care center.

Medications are also used to assist overcoming (psychological) addiction or decrease the harm resulting from it. Sometimes the practice of using specific medications for these purposes is discontinued, as with amphetamine or phen/fen for weight loss and hunger reduction, after substantial side effects are discovered. The medications shown below are some good initial options for overcoming addiction (but most who are successful in overcoming addiction do not use them). As you gain confidence, you can move on to psychological techniques for self-control:

⇒ Less harmful substitutes for the substance and/or method of delivery include methadone for heroin, and nicotine by patch/gum/spray/inhaler instead of from tobacco

⇒ For craving reduction: bromocriptine or amantadine for cocaine, naltrexone (ReVia) for alcohol, and naltrexone (Trexan) or LAAM for heroin. Acamprosate (Camprol), for alcohol, may also become approved for use in the U.S.

⇒ To make using extremely unlikely because it would be painful or fatal: disulfiram (Antabuse) for alcohol.

There is one additional way medication might be used, and that is to treat other psychological problems that contribute to addiction, such as depression, anxiety disorders, attention deficit disorder, schizophrenia and bipolar disorder. The results from using these medications range from dramatic success to no response. Side effects can also be a major factor in your willingness to continue them. Only by trying them will you know how much help they provide. The ultimate goal is to eliminate negative consequences of addiction (and other psychological problems) in your life. This process requires a number of steps. The final steps are psychological. Which step you start with doesn't matter if you are eventually successful.

Notes

11

Other Satisfactions

I can live better *without it*

Overview

Before you got involved with your addiction, you experienced other satisfactions. Even during your addiction there have been other satisfactions, but you may have overlooked their significance. If you overcome your addiction, you create the opportunity to experience even better and more satisfying experiences in life. Being productive, having good relationships, and accepting yourself can be especially satisfying. If thrills are still important to you, there are other ways (less risky than your addiction) to experience them.

Before And During Your Addiction There Were Other Satisfactions

You probably did not get involved with your addiction until at least your teens or twenties, and your involvement may not have become an addiction until some later time. During those pre-addiction years you almost certainly experienced satisfactions (pleasures, enjoyments, highs, euphorias, thrills). Many of those satisfactions were probably the ordinary ones of day-to-day life, such as eating, enjoying time with other people, games or sports, reading and learning, music, or work (at a job or at home). On occasion you may also have experienced special satisfactions that you still remember, such as a vacation, a trip to an amusement park, seeing a movie you really enjoyed, a visit with people you didn't get to see often, a special event, or other satisfying events.

There may have been significant pain in your life as well, and that pain may have influenced you to get involved with your addiction. However, it is important to recognize that your life had satisfaction even then. With luck, some of the examples in the preceding paragraph have activated memories of those satisfactions.

Even during your addiction you experienced some of the same day-to-day satisfactions and had occasional special ones. Because the high from addiction can be intense, it is easy to ignore the rest of life. You may have thought that without addiction "I can't get no satisfaction." To recognize that there are other satisfactions is to weaken the connection between yourself and the addiction.

Higher Satisfactions

Perhaps the primary problem of addiction is that although cravings and needs are satisfied by it, and problems after a fashion are coped with, the deeper needs and strivings, the ones which make us most human and most ourselves, tend to be ignored while we are addicted. There is some satisfaction in addiction, but there is higher satisfaction from addressing deeper needs.

As a small step, it is helpful to recognize that if you overcome your addiction, you are almost certain to increase your enjoyment of day-to-day satisfactions in life. Eating, sleeping, moving and walking, music and dance, talking with others, and observing nature, to name a few, can become much more enjoyable experiences. Your entire life can have a different feel to it!

An even better reason than the increase in day-to-day satisfaction is that you are also almost certain to experience other, even higher satisfactions. Although the high of addiction is intense, it is brief. Furthermore, an addictive high does not connect us, except perhaps momentarily, with others, and it does not give us an opportunity to develop our abilities. Higher satisfactions involve connections outside ourselves and growth in our abilities. When we pursue higher satisfactions, we also accept ourselves better, because we are acting on our ultimate goals and values.

Higher satisfactions come from enduring relationships with others and with productive activity. These relationships allow us to keep expanding our abilities and to overcome our inherent isolation as human beings. Having momentary satisfactions is also acceptable and desirable, but a primary focus on them leaves our lives lopsided. Achieving a balance between momentary and enduring satisfactions is a topic of the next chapter.

The term "opportunity cost" refers to what you miss out on when you place your resources here, not there. By spending my time watching television, I miss out on other activities that might have been more meaningful. Every activity has an opportunity cost. Even moderated involvement with a substance or activity involves time and often money. The involvement does not have significant costs (it is by definition moderation), but the resources it consumes are not available for something else.

Consider food choices. Candy and dessert do not provide the enduring nutrition that is the ultimate purpose of eating. They do provide something tasty, a brief pleasure, and energy which might be quickly expended. However, they (typically) do not provide the other nutrients needed to thrive. With addiction your life is oriented around candy and dessert, and your deeper needs are not being well fed. You are so full from candy and dessert that even when good food comes along, you don't have much appetite for it (opportunity cost). When you reduce the candy and dessert, over time you develop an appetite for foods which will feed your deeper needs. Even nutritious foods taste good, if you allow yourself time to get to know them and your taste buds are not overwhelmed by sweets.

Many of us look beyond connecting with others and productive work, as important as these are, to connecting with God or some spiritual being, or to developing our spiritual selves. I have wanted to make the case that even without a spiritual orientation, addiction is a violation of ourselves. Addiction would appear to be even more a violation of our spiritual selves.

When you have stopped having your "love affair" with addiction, you have the opportunity to have a real love affair with another individual. Because it is difficult to have two love affairs simultaneously, as long as you are addicted, a loving relationship with another individual cannot blossom. It blossoms when it is characterized by knowledge of one another, respect and caring for one another, and effort given for one another. In such a relationship it is perhaps even more important to give than to receive. The capacity to participate in such a relationship may be as high an accomplishment as one can achieve. A loving relationship that has blossomed is more satisfying than addiction, and without the negative consequences.

If you have children or grandchildren, you can experience the satisfaction of being with them and guiding them. There are also children almost everywhere who could benefit from more attention and guidance. Nieces and nephews, neighborhood children, and the children of friends are possibilities. Volunteer activities with children also abound. Contact local charities to discover specific opportunities. If you are knowledgeable in any sport, volunteer coaches and assistant coaches for youth sports leagues are always in demand. Start slowly and gradually. Don't force yourself on kids just because *you* now have the time. You'll feel even worse if you overcommit then retreat. But you may discover that you are willing and able to make children an important part of your life.

Caution: Depending on your addiction and its severity, working with children may not be appropriate until you have a sufficient history of success in overcoming your addiction. You need to think carefully about these issues. If you are volunteering through an organization, expect to make full disclosure of your past addictive activities, and to be closely supervised in your work.

There are numerous other types of relationships than can be meaningful and satisfying. We might even include relationships with pets and plants. Most of the time I was writing this workbook the family cat was curled up on the bed behind me. I think we both experienced a sense of connection. The satisfaction from relationships may not be as intense as the addictive high, but it is more enduring and without the costs of addiction.

In Chapter 6 I paraphrased Aristotle, who suggested that all individuals by nature desire to learn. This idea might be expanded to suggest that for all the variability of human beings, there are some enduring aspects, a "human nature." This human nature includes, Aristotle suggests, a motivation to keep expanding one's abilities and powers and knowledge. For some individuals addiction is a reaction to having been blocked in the opportunity to grow in these ways (or to the loss of a relationship). For all, however, overcoming addiction allows for a greater opportunity for learning. Acting on this opportunity improves life as well as prevents relapse. It is time to learn! Time to do, study, practice, work, read, listen, work out, ask questions, reflect, get coached, take classes!

Accepting Yourself

Completing a workbook might not be enough to help you overcome addiction if you have a significantly distorted sense of yourself. However, I do hope to persuade you to identify distortions in your self-understanding and challenge them. Psychotherapy is an excellent way to challenge these distortions, and I hope you will consider it if you have them.

The simplest way to identify inaccuracies in your self-understanding is to ask whether you have any broad negative conclusions about or descriptions of your abilities or worth. Specific conclusions and descriptions are usually not a problem. For instance, you might say about yourself, "I don't know how to speak French, or how to rebuild an engine, or how to play baseball." These are (for most people) factual statements. You may regret these facts, but you can change them if you are motivated to do so. These facts are also balanced by other facts, like being able to play the piano or being a good listener or good cook.

But you might say about your abilities, "I can't learn languages," or "I can't learn new things," or "I don't know how to do very much." These are *sweeping negative generalizations*. They have exceptions that make them untrue, but you ignore these exceptions. Of course, there will be some truth in these statements also, but in your generalizations "some truth" has been raised to the "whole truth." Once you accept these statements as the whole truth, it can be difficult to change them because your belief may prevent you from recognizing or seeking out facts that might contradict it. Your belief may become a self-fulfilling prophecy.

You might also say, about yourself and your worth, "I am no good; I will never amount to anything; It is impossible for me to be happy." I would not agree with these statements for anyone. These statements may be based on specific episodes of misguided behavior or lack of success or periods of depression, but the facts have been exaggerated. These beliefs can also become self-fulfilling prophecies.

Besides considering psychotherapy, and the self-help books in Chapter 6 on depression and self-esteem, I suggest that you also recall your history. These kinds of negative beliefs usually do not arise from within us, but from outside of us. Human beings do not normally have negative beliefs about self unless they are taught to have them.

Imagine the following scenario. Every day from birth until age 18 a child is told negative things ("You're bad. You'll never amount to anything. You're stupid. You're ugly."). Furthermore, the child is treated without affection or interest. At age 18, inquire about this individual's self-concept and self-acceptance. What do you find?

The answer is obvious. Although this individual may develop self-acceptance later, there will be much work to do. Fortunately few children are raised in this consistently demeaning way. Many, however, are raised in a way that alternates between being demeaned and being supported. Sometimes the demeaning episodes go beyond verbal abuse to include physical and sexual abuse. Although parents or primary caretakers may be the main causes of being demeaned, others may contribute. Some individuals may sincerely believe that demeaning treatment is good motivation. Most may simply not have risen above the treatment they themselves received.

Inaccurate beliefs about yourself, and about others and the world (which also develop in a demeaning environment), can lead to addiction as well as general unhappiness. For instance, you may believe that by yourself you cannot manage your own emotions and that you can do so only with the help of an addiction. You may believe that all positive experiences ultimately end in misfortune, or that others are not to be trusted. With these kinds of beliefs, escape into addiction may seem desirable. In turn your addiction may seem to confirm your negative sense of yourself.

On the one hand addiction can help you escape the pain of past experience and the pain of experiencing your negative view of yourself, and on the other it can lead to more pain and more evidence that you really are "no good." It is necessary to attack both sides of this experience. You need to cope with negative past experiences and negative beliefs and to overcome addiction.

Regardless of how you were treated, and regardless of whatever genetic factors or misfortunes you have suffered, the task of challenging and modifying your self-concept is to rise above these factors, because they are past and unchangeable. What can be done now is to transform your beliefs ("there is nothing either good or bad but thinking makes it so"). I emphasize considering your history because perhaps doing so will help you realize that anyone who had experienced what you have experienced might have similar beliefs and a similar sense of relief from addiction. If you had a different set of experiences, you probably would have a different set of beliefs. What ends up on the inside starts on the outside. Now that you are old enough to have more control of the outside, and to examine mistaken beliefs and modify them, you can start re-shaping the inside. One of the first and most important steps that you can take, as discussed in Chapter 6, is to spend more time around individuals who like and accept you as you are, and less around those who don't.

Having Thrills

Some individuals develop addictions in part because they are particularly interested in thrills (highly arousing experiences). Many individuals enjoy riding fast in a car, but for thrill seekers, only a Ferrari at top speed will suffice. The desire for thrills is not bad in itself. This desire only becomes problematic when the thrills are particularly dangerous or harmful.

Every activity in life involves a certain degree of risk, and we each perform our own risk/benefit analysis of the activities we engage in. For instance, most people choose to ride on streets and freeways, even though there is a risk of accident and injury. Some ordinary activities are more risky than being on the street, others less so. However, all activities involve some degree of risk. We each choose the level of risk we are willing to accept, and the level of thrill we find enjoyable.

If thrills are important to you, you might consider skydiving, hang gliding, auto racing, boxing, scuba diving, martial arts, flying, platform diving, sailplaning, bungee jumping, skiing, ski jumping, wilderness adventures, or rock climbing, to name a few. Less obvious but possibly equally good opportunities might be public speaking, musical or theatrical performance, or other public performance activities.

If you decide to overcome your addiction, you do not necessarily need to give up thrills. It may be valuable for you to begin to seek them out. Once you realize the abundant opportunities for experiencing them, addiction may be easier to let go of.

Regardless of whether you are regularly experiencing thrills or only less intense but still higher satisfactions, the point to overcoming addiction is to have a better life, not a deprived and boring one. The whole point to this workbook is:

You can live better *without it*. Although many think of addiction as a moral problem, I suggest that it is primarily a practical one. Addiction gets in the way of accomplishing what you really want to do. It's not time to stop getting high; it's time to find better ways to get high.

Questions . . .

1. What significant satisfactions did you experience before your addiction?

2. What significant satisfactions have you experienced during your addiction? To what extent might you have underestimated the significance of these satisfactions because of your focus on the addiction?

3. What satisfactions will you quickly have the opportunity to experience if you overcome the addiction?

4. If you overcome the addiction, what satisfactions might you be able to experience once you have prepared sufficiently for them?

5. What are the greatest nonaddiction highs and satisfactions that you can imagine yourself experiencing? What would be involved in moving you closer in the direction of experiencing them?

6. What work or activities are you especially good at? If you are tempted to answer "nothing," because you are comparing yourself to others, then compare yourself only to yourself. What activities are *your* best, regardless of how you compare to others who do them?

7. What assistance or resources would you need to improve on your abilities in these areas? How motivated are you to make these improvements? If you made these improvements, how satisfying do you think they would be?

8. What are the most important relationships in your life?

9. What do you need to do to repair or improve each of these relationships?

10. To what extent do you accept yourself as you are? If not fully, what would need to change in yourself in order to accept yourself?

11. What experiences in your upbringing were crucial in shaping your degree of acceptance of yourself?

12. To what extent has addiction been a way to escape the pain of past experience?

13. If self-acceptance is difficult for you, which individuals do you need to spend more time with (because they like and accept you), and which do you need to spend less time with?

14. To what extent do you consider yourself a thrill seeker? What thrills would you like to experience at least once? Which ones would you like to have regularly in your life?

15. What would you most like to learn about or learn how to do?

Projects . . .

1. Pick a satisfying activity from your pre-addiction life. To the extent possible, engage again in this activity. How satisfying is it now?

2. Attempt to have a day in which there are no extraordinary satisfactions, only the satisfactions of daily living. How do you feel at the end of this day? How do you sleep that night?

3. Pick a satisfying activity that you could readily do, and that you have considered doing before, but you held back from because of your addiction. Do that activity soon. How satisfying is it?

4. Make an effort to improve on one of your best abilities. How satisfying is this experience?

5. Pick one of your important relationships, and do something simple to improve it. For instance, set aside time to listen to this individual, and to understand his or her views on something. Or, help the individual to perform a task that you could be of assistance on. How satisfying is this experience?

6. If there is a child or teenager you can spend some time with, arrange to do that. (Please note "caution" earlier in this chapter.) How easily does the child or teenager accept your attention? How satisfying is the encounter?

7. Identify moments when you are not accepting yourself, and record simple observations about them as they occur. For instance, the who, what, when, where, and why of the experience. After you have collected several of these observations, do you perceive any patterns in them? What courses of action do these patterns suggest?

8. Identify moments when you do feel accepting of yourself, and record the same simple observations about them as they occur. What patterns do you perceive, and what courses of action do these patterns suggest?

9. If you are interested in experiencing thrills, identify one and experience it. How did the experience compare with your expectations?

10. Set aside one or two hours, pick some knowledge or skill that you would like to have, and learn it, or as much of it as you can in that brief time period. How satisfying is it to act on your curiosity in this way?

What's Important Now?

If you date your answers to these questions, the answers over time will become a diary of your growth. It is likely that in future readings of this chapter different ideas will be important to you, reflecting the fact that you are indeed changing.

Which ideas from this chapter are most useful *to you, now*?

How can you put these ideas into action?

How much confidence do you have in your judgement in selecting these ideas as crucial at this time? (Circle a number; 10 is highest confidence)

0   1   2   3   4   5   6   7   8   9   10

12

Building A New Life

*As we become permanent drunkards by so many separate drinks,
so we become saints in the moral, and authorities and experts in
the practical and scientific spheres, by so many separate acts and
hours of work. Let no youth have any anxiety about the upshot of
his education, whatever the line of it may be. If he keep faithfully
busy each hour of the working day, he may safely leave the final
result to itself. He can with perfect certainty count on waking up
some fine morning, to find himself one of the competent ones of
his generation, in whatever pursuit he may have singled out.*
-- William James (1842-1910)
The Principles of Psychology, 1890

Overview

You can build a new life that is even more satisfying than life with your
addiction. The more severe your addiction, the more different your new life will
be. During the initial period of overcoming addiction your primary focus will be
on coping with craving. As craving diminishes your focus will shift to building
habits which reflect your ultimate goals and values, and which enable you to
experience the satisfactions that arise from these goals and values. Building good
habits (positive addictions) involves observing the (good and not so good) habits
of others, persistently but patiently taking small steps, revising behavior as
needed to solve problems or fit larger goals, and looking beyond short-term
difficulties to the long-term results you want. Your new life will also need a
balance between momentary and higher satisfactions. Good health habits
establish a foundation for other satisfactions.

Major Problems Require Major Changes, but It's Worth It

As we discussed in Chapter 7, you have a choice about whether to continue or overcome your addiction. You probably would not choose to overcome it if you thought your life would be as bad or even worse after the change. You also might not choose to change if you thought you were not capable of change. Why try to do something that is not possible for you?

I hope that this workbook is persuading you that change is possible for you, by showing you how to make the change. I mentioned in Chapter 3 that change involves wanting to do something and knowing how to do it. Both are required. Chapters 3 through 5 helped you identify why you would want to change. The remaining chapters present ideas and techniques you can use to make the change. I hope that among the many ideas and techniques I have presented are the ones you have been missing. As I mentioned at the end of Chapter 6, you are probably only missing a few pieces of this puzzle, not all of them. I hope this workbook is helping you find the missing pieces.

The more severe your addiction, the more change will be necessary for you in order to achieve a new life, one which is satisfying and not at significant risk of relapsing back to addiction. Of course, only you can decide if this new life is worth it. However, Chapter 5 helped you identify the costs of your addiction. How much do you want to keep experiencing these? Won't your life clearly be better if you could eliminate or reduce these problems?

Focus On Cravings First, Then Build Good Habits

During your initial change efforts, craving will probably be the primary issue. The techniques in Chapter 10 can help you to endure these cravings without acting on them and outlast them until over weeks or months they die away.

Once craving significantly diminishes, the initial battle has been won. Your primary focus then needs to become building good habits (positive addictions). You can be building good habits from the beginning, but once the craving is lower it will be easier. If cravings do occur later on, re-directing your attention to your good habit is one way to cope.

Addiction can be thought of as bad habit. If you eliminate this bad habit, you will be creating a vacuum, an empty spot in your life. Nature abhors a vacuum. If you do not fill this vacuum with something new (like a good habit, a positive addiction), there is a significant risk that the addiction will return. For instance, if you end all your friendships because your friends have not been good to you, but you do not develop new friendships, you will get lonely. As your loneliness increases, it will be increasingly easy to go back to your old friends.

Chapter 1 suggested that overcoming a (negative) addiction goes hand in hand with developing a positive addiction (or good habit). Any repeated action that serves your ultimate goals and values is a good habit. I suggested earlier that by living in accordance with your ultimate goals and values, you increase the chances for being happy.

To review (from Chapter 7), the ultimate aim in life is happiness. Ultimate goals are those which are (thought to be) the last step before happiness ("I want to be rich, because if I'm rich I'll be happy"). Values are the guidelines and preferences we live by ("I'm going to be rich, but I'm going to do it honestly"). The myriad levels of goals, values, habits and other behaviors and beliefs are different levels of means to the ultimate end of happiness. In the last chapter we focused on higher satisfactions. In this chapter we focus lower down on this ladder of happiness, the rung of good habits. Good habits lead to the opportunity to experience the satisfactions of your goals, as you live in accordance with your values. Good habits are the foundation of higher satisfactions.

Having achieved or come close to an ultimate goal, we may also develop a different perspective on it. One might realize, for instance, that focusing on being rich was actually an effort to be accepted and loved. Upon satisfying a desire we in time grow bored and move on. With luck we move higher, to a higher desire prompting us to a higher satisfaction. Desire and satisfaction mature hand in hand. (This is Freud's "sublimation" or Socrates's "ladder of love.") However we describe this kind of maturation, when we are surrendered to addiction, not much maturation occurs.

Imagine that your ultimate goal, as you understand yourself, is to serve others. You believe that serving others will give you the best happiness you can imagine. This goal is related to your value that human life is more important than anything else you can think of. In order to serve others, you will need to have something of value to them. Based on your natural talents, suppose that you decide to become a teacher. In order to become a good teacher, one who truly can serve others, you will need a variety of good habits. These good habits will assure that your preparation to become a teacher and your efforts as a teacher, will be effective.

By developing your awareness of your goals, and pursuing them, you will not be happy all the time, or necessarily perfectly happy ever. But you might experience such happiness as human beings may experience from time to time. Contrast that experience with addiction, which is a fleeting "glimpse of paradise" combined with costs that can be substantial or even horrendous. What do *you* conclude?

If you are unsure about what good habits to develop, there is guidance available from your answers to the Questions in Chapters 4 and 6, which help you identify problems with which you need to cope; and the Questions in Chapter 7, which ask you about your ultimate goals and values. For instance, if in Chapter 4 you indicated that addiction was a way to cope with anger, then you need new good habits for coping with anger. What I did not say in Chapter 6 (Coping & Connecting) but add now, is that one way to think of a coping method is that it is a good habit. Thus the information about building good habits, in this chapter, goes along with the information in Chapter 6. Similarly, if in Chapter 7 you answered that one of your goals or sub-goals is having your own business, then you need to work on having the skills and habits necessary to achieving this goal.

Building Good Habits

A habit is a bundle of other behaviors or skills. It is a series of steps, done without much conscious effort because the series has been done so often. A habit can be as small as the sequence someone uses to read sections of the newspaper, or as large as the steps taken to prepare a complicated meal. In order to have a habit you need to be able to perform the skills involved at each step. The first step in building some habits, therefore, is learning the component skills. You can already open different sections of a newspaper. You may not yet have the cooking skills to emulate a master chef's way of making a particular meal.

Having selected some habits or skills to develop, how might you proceed? The following set of related suggestions may be helpful to you. They can be applied in many different ways as you overcome addiction.

◆ **Find models and teachers.** As noted in Chapter 6, watching and interacting with others is how we learn almost everything. Not only do we learn behaviors, skills, and habits from others, we also discover which ones we want to learn. In addition to learning what is necessary to pursue your goals and be consistent with your values, also study others to find out what you want to do (or not do). Watch them when you can, and ask questions if possible. As also noted in Chapter 6, you can even interact with others by reading their books or similar presentations. Probably every significant skill or behavior that exists has at least one book written about it. In other words, you are not alone.

◆ **Take small steps.** This principle suggests that in building any new skill or behavior into your life, you need to work one small step at a time. For instance, if you are not a runner, it would be unwise and unrealistic to begin your exercise program by attempting to run three miles on a Monday morning. Small steps to take might include getting a physical exam, buying new shoes, getting up regularly at that time (if it is earlier than before), finding a partner, reading a book on running, doing other exercises to strengthen the muscles used in running, walking at first, alternating jogging and walking, and so forth.

◆ **Persist.** As William James noted (the opening quotation of this chapter), if you keep faithfully busy, the final result will happen in time. This means that you will need to be patient about your progress on a day-to-day basis. Slow, gradual progress brought on by regular attention and effort is much more likely to stay with you than are sudden bursts of effort that can also suddenly fade away. Particularly in the first month or two of a new habit, daily attention is needed. Part of what we mean by "habit" is that the behavior occurs without much conscious effort. You will only get to that "auto-pilot" level with regular repetition. Once you are there, you will again have more attention available to develop the next habit you want to work on. Life is a series of habit-building experiences. If you take control of the process, you will build the kind of life you want to have.

◆ **Be mindful.** It is not enough to go through the motions of developing skills and habits. You need to consider carefully every step taken, study the details, and think about where everything is headed. Your behaviors also need to be pieced into a bigger picture. The biggest picture is framed by your goals and values. There may be times when a minor or major change is indicated. For instance, if there are significant problems that arise in following through on your running program, it is time not only to consider how to solve these problems, but also to consider alternative forms of exercise. The big picture is probably about getting exercise, not about running itself. Similarly, there is an even bigger picture than exercise. Perhaps running in the morning means you don't get enough sleep, which, of course, causes other problems. It may be better to exercise at a different time. Mindlessly pursuing running, or not pursuing it because problems have arisen, or pursuing it to the detriment of other goals, does not fit the bigger picture.

◆ **Stay motivated by maintaining perspective.** Just as with overcoming addiction, in the process of developing skills and habits, you can experience slips and relapses. When this happens with addiction, it is time to recall your cost-benefit analysis, the reasons why you decided to change. The same is true for other behavior change. If your day-to-day life is consistent with your goals and values, then you are in fact working on the vision you have for yourself. When you slip off track, recall where you ultimately want to be, and consider the behaviors needed to get you there. Although there may be discomfort involved with building habits and skills (just like coping with craving!), that discomfort is worth it, because it allows you to accomplish your goals. Keeping a long-term perspective will keep you motivated to cope with the immediate discomforts you are facing.

◆ **Make a pledge.** I mention this suggestion because it is commonly mentioned in the context of habit change. However, I suggest caution. For some individuals making an announcement about change can be helpful. Unfortunately, such an announcement may lead to thinking that overcoming addiction is done in part to please the recipients of the announcement. As I suggested in Question 9, Chapter 10, selfish motivation for change is likely to work best. Making a pledge, either about a habit change or about overcoming addiction, may be counterproductive for you. Probably making a pledge works best when developing socially approved behaviors, rather than overcoming socially disapproved behaviors.

Balance

Addiction centers on the pursuit of momentary satisfaction. This chapter has identified how to build up your capacity to pursue satisfaction over the long term. Your life needs a balance between momentary and long-term satisfactions.

You could put all your money into savings or retirement (the long-term focus), or all of it into day-to-day spending (which would be akin to addiction). With literally all your money in savings, you might starve in a week. If all of it goes to immediate spending, you have no reserves. Balance is necessary.

For some individuals addiction has been a way to balance an unbalanced life. If you rush around under great stress all day or all week, with little time to yourself and little momentary satisfaction, then when evening or the weekend arrives, it is finally "your time." Devoting "your time" to addiction may just compound the stress the next day or week. Alternative coping methods can certainly be employed each night or weekend, and not engaging in the addiction will probably also make the next day or week better. However, getting a better balance in daily and weekly life might be the primary solution. Working hard on your job is important to your long term goals, but a focus on work to the extent that it regularly impairs your day-to-day well-being is counterproductive.

Achieving a day-to-day balance is also an important aspect of preventing relapse. Balance in life, like actual physical balance (for instance, doing a handstand) involves small movements around a balance point, not adopting a fixed position. As you develop balance in life, the movement to either side of your balance point can become smaller, as you become more skillful in maintaining balance. Being mindful of bigger perspectives will also help you realize that at times your life may become quite unbalanced in one respect, for the sake of achieving balance from a larger perspective. For instance, taking money from savings to buy something needed for an important project disrupts your daily balance of spending money, but it may restore a balance between investing in the your future (savings) and investing in your present (the project).

A simple method for achieving day-to-day balance is to have a daily and weekly schedule. Consider the following (overlapping) categories of lifestyle balance. By scheduling adequate time for:
⇒ Work and relaxation
⇒ Activity and contemplation (self-assessment)
⇒ Duties and fun
⇒ Long term projects and momentary pleasure
⇒ Alone time and social time
⇒ Routine household chores and new projects
⇒ "Shoulds" and "wants"
⇒ Making money and spending money
⇒ Spiritual time and secular time
⇒ Giving and receiving
⇒ Being physically distant and being physically close
⇒ Exercise and rest
⇒ Personal maintenance (see "good health habits" below) and productivity
⇒ Going fast and going slow
⇒ Learning from others and learning independently

You greatly increase the chances that as the day and week unfold you will be feeling satisfied with your life. Each individual will have a different balance on these opposites. Over time you will learn how best to balance them for yourself.

For now a significant portion of time may need to be devoted to thinking about overcoming addiction. This time might include reading, attending treatment or support groups, monitoring different behaviors and reflecting on them, developing new coping methods, and so forth. Eventually you will overcome your addiction (if you work at it persistently!), and this time will be available for other projects and satisfactions.

Develop Good Health Habits

One of the ironies of the modern age is that we are living it in Stone-Age bodies. Our genetic constitution has changed very little in the last few hundred thousand years, but our environments have changed dramatically.

Imagine that a Stone-Age adult is magically transported into the Modern age, and magically taught to communicate. Here is what I would tell this individual about how to live healthily in the modern era:

1. *Get enough sleep.* There is still much activity going on after the sun goes down, and it can be hard to ignore. Spending some quiet time before going to bed may help you fall asleep.

2. *Eat well, but not too much.* Much modern food is mostly manufactured. It's worth the effort to find the whole foods you are used to eating. In your pre-chocolate world, taste was a good guide to what was nutritious. Now the taste may be manufactured in as the nutrients are removed. Food is so plentiful that it's easy to overeat. Gorging yourself may have been wise when you didn't know when you might eat again, but now it will just lead to being overweight.

3. *Wash your hands frequently.* You were used to coming into contact with the same small group of people, and you got used to each other's germs. Now you could come into contact, directly or indirectly, with hundreds of people every day.

4. *Take care of your teeth.* Your old diet may have protected you from dental problems more than a modern diet. You are also going to live longer, so you'll need your teeth longer.

5. *Exercise and stretch.* You used to get exercise just by leading your daily life, but now you'll need to make it part of your schedule. Even though you usually don't need to be strong and flexible to survive anymore, you'll feel better, prevent injuries, and be thinner.

6. *Get rest and relaxation.* It is easy to get caught up in work and various stimulating but shallow modern activities. In your world there weren't many possessions to obtain, and no slot machines. If you regularly overwork or get over-stimulated, you may turn outside yourself for help to calm down and thereby reduce your natural ability to do this.

7. *Stay connected to others and to nature.* In your world you were surrounded by others you knew well. The land, plants, animals and the elements were integral to your daily life. Now you will often be surrounded by strangers and may have much less contact with nature. Modern science is now verifying that connections to others and to nature are also important to health, even though we are unclear why. Nurture your relationships, and maintain some contact with mother earth.

Fortunately, it is possible to live much better today than in the Stone Age. The self-disciplines just described will establish a foundation of health so that you can make the most of the modern world.

Questions . . .

1. If you accomplish all of the changes in your life that you have been considering, what are the main ways your life will be different?

2. If you have already begun overcoming your addiction, how strong is craving for you at this time? How much energy do you have to identify and build new habits?

3. Much material has been covered since you answered these questions in Chapter 7, so it may be time to ask them again: What are your ultimate goals? What sub-goals are needed to be in position to accomplish these goals? What are your most deeply held values?

4. What do you think will be most satisfying as you achieve each of the goals listed above?

5. How happy do you think you will be if you achieve your goals? How happy do you think you will be on the way there?

6. What skills and good habits are you most interested in developing now?

7. How are these skills and good habits related to your goals?

8. What problems will you need to overcome to develop these skills and habits?

9. Recall an example of your being persistent about something. Describe the ways you were persistent. How hard was it to do these things? Was it worth it?

10. Recall an example of facing a problem, and shifting from a smaller perspective (I need to run) to a larger one (I need exercise). How were you able to accomplish this shift? Did others around you have more difficulty making this shift?

11. What is your experience with making pledges about changes you are making? Based on this experience, how helpful or unhelpful is making a pledge (about a habit change, about overcoming addiction) likely to be?

12. What aspects of your life seem particularly out of balance? What changes in your daily or weekly schedule might be needed?

13. How much regular time do you need to devote to overcoming addiction at this point?

14. Which of the good health habits listed above need more of your attention and effort?

Projects . . .

1. Observe, as well as you can, the small and large habits of someone you admire. If possible, ask why these habits occur as they do. What do you discover that you would like to include in your own life?

2. Observe, as well as you can, the small and large habits of someone whose behavior seems less than admirable. What do you discover that you would like to include or not include in your own life?

3. Identify someone who has a specific skill or habit that you would like to develop. Observe this individual in action, and ask questions if possible. What do you learn?

4. In Question 6 above you indicated the skills and habits you are most interested in learning now. What small steps could you take now for each of them? Do these small steps. What did you learn from this experience?

What's Important Now?

If you date your answers to these questions, the answers over time will become a diary of your growth. It is likely that in future readings of this chapter different ideas will be important to you, reflecting the fact that you are indeed changing.

Which ideas from this chapter are most useful *to you, now*?

How can you put these ideas into action?

How much confidence do you have in your judgement in selecting these ideas as crucial at this time? (Circle a number; 10 is highest confidence)

0   1   2   3   4   5   6   7   8   9   10

13

Following Through

It's easy to quit. I've done it dozens of times.

Overview

Regardless of whether they have been written down, you have some plans for addressing your addiction. Reviewing your plans regularly will keep them as a focus of your attention. You can notice a slip or relapse well before it actually happens. When you first notice a slip or relapse on the way, review your motivations for overcoming addiction. All relapses start as slips, but a slip does not have to become a relapse. If you follow through successfully, in time the process of following through on change, and the process of living your life, will become identical. When you arrive at this point you will have overcome addiction!

Plans to Change, Written And Unwritten

Perhaps one of the shortcomings of this workbook is that I have not pushed you to commit to any specific plan or timeframe for overcoming your addiction. Right or wrong, this omission was deliberate. You have been invited at the end of Chapters 7 and 10 to write plans for overcoming addiction and to act on them. You will again be invited to do so at the end of this chapter. At the end of each chapter you have also been invited to write down the ideas from the chapter you considered most useful and to consider how to put these ideas into action. These end-of-chapter questions are a way of updating your plans as you progress through the workbook. However, at no point have I confronted you with "now is the time, what are you going to do, and when are you going to do it?"

Regardless of whether I suggest that you make one, I believe you already have plans about your addiction and some timeframe for acting on them. Reading this workbook may already be part of larger plans you made before getting the workbook. Or you may be waiting to finish the workbook before deciding what to do next. Many other plans are possible, because there is an infinite variety of individuals and life circumstances.

Rather than occurring through one master plan, I believe addiction changes as the result of a collection of plans. It's not often a very organized collection either, in my experience. Overcoming addiction is not like constructing a building, where before you begin you carefully think out the floor plan and the construction methods. With addiction, by the time you have a good sense of the final outcome and how you are going to get there, you are already pretty much there! I am optimistic that you will get there, but I am acknowledging the reality that you may for now be unsure about exactly how all the changes, or even which changes, will occur.

For instance, you may be confident that for now abstinence is a better choice than moderation, and that you need to learn how to cope with work stress better so that you can stop your addiction and not feel completely stressed out once it's gone. Until you figure out the stress problem, you don't think stopping is a good idea. However, you feel stuck about how you are going to figure it out. You may also think that relationship issues are part of the picture, but you're not sure how they fit in. Lastly, you are not sure you want to be in this job to start with, so why try to reduce the stress there? Maybe looking for another job would make more sense? Still, you think you a have big role in your work stress, because of the attitudes you have, and you don't want to take bad attitudes to a new job. Who knows, a new job could be even more stressful!

That's your plan. You know where you want to go, sort of, but you don't know how to get there exactly, partly because you are not even sure of all the problems that need to be solved. I believe that having stated one sub-problem (I need to figure out how to reduce stress) will make it more likely that you will focus on it and solve it. I suggested in Chapter 2 that the primary reason that you still had an addiction was that you had not focused yourself on solving it. That may still be true, but now it may be sub-problems, not the main problem, that are in the way. There is also the issue of prioritizing problems. Should the primary focus be stress reduction or getting a new job? You won't know if you don't focus on those questions.

There is a time-honored description of problem solving: identify the problem, gather information about it, select and try out a solution, observe how well the solution works and make adjustments as needed. There are few problems that actually get solved this simply, but the steps are still helpful to keep in mind. Usually we keep redefining what the problem is, partly because of new information and partly because as we think about it our perspective on it may change.

I do think it is helpful to write down whatever plans you have currently, however unconnected and disorganized they seem. If you are unsure about making the effort to do this, recall that human memory is not the most secure place to record something important. However, what I most encourage you to do is to be fully aware of your plans, possibly by saying them out loud. I mentioned earlier that brain systems don't always communicate so well. Speaking out loud seems to help communication. Maybe by going out and coming back in again the message is taken more seriously! Given how our brains seem to function, with a less than complete coordination in many areas, perhaps it should be no surprise that master plans are not that frequent in human behavior.

Whatever your plans, they summarize your best estimate of where you are going, why you are going, how you are getting there, and what problems remain to be solved. If you review your plans regularly you will stay aware of them, and be in a better position to move forward on them and change them as needed. A simple way to do this is to review regularly the last section of each chapter, "What's Important Now?"

Although your plans aim toward a happier future, you may still be hindered by the excesses of your past. Just because you overcome an addiction does not mean you immediately get past the negative consequences of your previous behavior. You may now be devoting significant effort to getting out of debt, restoring your health, reestablishing relationships, coping with legal issues, and so forth. If your addiction began early in life, you may also be doing remedial work. When addiction begins early, we may not fully mature. Consequently, you may also be devoting significant effort to developing adequate self-discipline, a stable identity, and the capacity for emotional self-regulation. In short, you might have much to do right now. It could be hard to get all these activities into one coordinated master plan!

An alternative perspective to this idea that change occurs through a collection of plans is the idea that one master plan should be in place from the beginning. According to this view there should at least be a plan for abstinence (or perhaps moderation), and then everything else can be worked out later. I have no objection to this idea, if you agree with it. If you are willing to make a plan like this, without knowing how you will cope without your addiction, then I assume your addiction is quite mild. But if you truly rely on your addiction for coping, then you won't want to give it up until you are confident about what life will be like without it. It may take a while for that confidence to build. Once confidence is strong enough, you may be ready to make a master plan, but by then the project is almost over.

This last workbook chapter focuses on the possibility that, even if you are fully aware of your plans, you may at times not be moving forward on them, but moving backwards. This backwards movement, a slip or a relapse, is common. Fortunately, a slip or relapse can help you re-discover why you had made plans in the first place and strengthen your motivation to follow through completely.

Before we focus on following through completely, let's review. This workbook has attempted to guide you in overcoming addiction by presenting a large set of ideas, some of which — with luck — will help you. You may now be acting on or thinking about new ways to increase and maintain your motivation, connect with others, cope with craving, develop new coping methods, experience higher satisfactions, and build a new life. In short, you have some plans.

If you have already managed to construct a "master plan," congratulations! If so, then your actions to overcome addiction could be compared to a precision machine in which many parts work together to produce one final outcome. On the other hand, your approach to overcoming addiction may seem like a set of parts that are supposed to fit together but don't seem to. Either way, you need to prevent backtracking. Whether you have a coordinated plan or a set of plans in hope of coordination, you need to follow through.

Slips And Relapses

A slip (a momentary difficulty following through on a plan) or a relapse (a longer difficulty following through) can usually be observed well before it happens. Typically, changes in your emotions, behavior, thinking, and relationships all occur well before the actual slip. For instance, if one of the benefits of your addiction was to cope with anxiety, then a steadily increasing sense of fearfulness and anxiety could be a sign that you are about to slip. If you used to engage in your addiction in a certain part of town, and you now find yourself closer and closer to going there again, this could be a sign of an impending slip. You might find yourself starting to think that your addiction wasn't so bad after all. You might begin to notice a trend in your relationships such that you are spending more time with old addiction friends or making new friends who are just like them.

Behaviors that lead in the direction of a slip, but which may be rationalized at first, are known by several acronyms: AIDs (Apparently Irrelevant Decisions), SIDs (Seemingly Irrelevant Decisions) or SUBTLE (Seemingly Unimportant Behavior That Leads to Errors). What they all mean is that with practice and a willingness to watch for it, you can usually "see trouble comin' from a long ways off."

Although you may attempt to rationalize or explain away these signs to yourself or others, it can soon be obvious where these changes in your feelings, behaviors, thinking, or relationships are ultimately headed. Sometimes the slip is not obvious to you until after it has happened. If you learn from it, you will be able to see the next one coming from farther away. A slip is the last domino in a line of dominoes. It is possible to see the line of dominoes beginning to fall, and make changes well before the last one falls. Whether you notice the slip before or after it occurs, you have a choice: You can go back to the addiction, or you can keep moving forward in your life. A slip doesn't have to turn into a relapse.

When you begin to notice a slip headed your way, it is a good time to review Chapters 3, 4, and 5, and the reasons that you have for overcoming addiction. If you truly want to go back to the life you had with your addiction, you certainly can do so, but do you really want this?

Any skill or activity that you do not practice regularly will get out of practice, "rusty." Coping with craving is such a skill. As we discussed in Chapter 10, it is useful to bring out cravings regularly. Not only do you stay in practice, but, so to speak, you drain away any craving energy that might be building up and heading toward a slip.

Many individuals experience one or more slips during the course of changing an addiction. Research suggests that they are most common during the first 90 days after having made a change, but they can occur at any time. Slips are not recommended, of course, and with luck you can accomplish change without slips. However, a slip is not necessarily a disaster. When a slip occurs, you have a valuable opportunity for experiencing again the negative consequences of your addiction, as well as a reduction in the quality of your new life. As we have mentioned, craving activates only good memories of the addiction. If you have not engaged in the addiction for a while, and you have not been reviewing the benefits of overcoming it, your memory of the negatives may be dimmer. A slip can improve your memory substantially. Perhaps the slip also helps clarify how important new coping methods are, or the importance of becoming more deeply connected to others.

Even if you slip or relapse many times, with each effort at changing your addiction, you can learn more and more. Many individuals conclude that if backtracks have occurred, then overcoming addiction is not going to happen. The best predictor of the future is the past, right? I suggest an alternative interpretation. If you understand your backtracks you are in a better position to prevent those ways of backtracking from reoccurring. After you have had several backtracks, you may be running out of ways to have them! After enough trial-and-error learning, you have made all the errors, and success is what's left.

How to Tell You're Improving

Because it can take a while to change completely, it can be helpful to measure your progress along the way. Otherwise, you may not be sure you are improving!

Compare yourself from the time you started this project, until now, on the following factors:

⇒ Level of involvement with your addiction
⇒ Level of negative consequences
⇒ Overall quality of life (level of satisfaction)
⇒ Level of self-awareness
⇒ Level of self-acceptance
⇒ Use of alternative coping methods
⇒ Ability to identify problems and make changes to solve them
⇒ Quality of relationships
⇒ Willingness to be open with trusted others
⇒ Frequency, intensity and length of cravings
⇒ Length of time between slips
⇒ Length of relapses
⇒ Level of balance in life
⇒ Ability to describe goals and values

How to Know When You Have Overcome Addiction

In Chapter 6 we discussed how developing alternative coping methods would mean that you no longer needed the addiction. If addiction once made you feel confident, you might have taken a series of steps to cut down or stop addictive involvement and simultaneously build up your confidence in other ways. At first you probably had to cope with craving and work hard at practicing new ways of thinking, feeling and acting confidently. Over time being confident became second nature, and cravings went away. Now, as a result of being confident and not being dragged down by the addiction, your whole life has changed. You speak your thoughts, you treat yourself with respect (and others generally do also), you move forward on goals that are important to you, and you have already achieved quite a few. Now, addiction isn't needed and isn't appealing either: You have too much to lose.

You just reviewed a list of indications that progress was occurring, that you were overcoming addiction. Now review a similar list, but one which shows you that addiction has been overcome:

⇒ Leading your life is its own reward
⇒ A return to addiction looks bad rather than good
⇒ Significant cravings are an experience of the past
⇒ Whatever you got through addiction you now get by less costly (and better) methods
⇒ Your life is balanced and stable

⇒ Your relationships are close and getting closer
⇒ You are productive and even creative
⇒ You are conceiving and moving toward even higher satisfactions
If this list sounds like you, then you have overcome addiction! You don't need to do anything to focus on overcoming addiction anymore. For perhaps a long time you had taken many steps, acted on many plans, and solved many problems. But now there is nothing left to do. Your life as you lead it is your relapse prevention plan. Simply by living as you live you are following through on overcoming addiction.

Questions . . .

1. Consider whether you have plans or a master plan. Which perspective seems more accurate for you?

2. How many slips or relapses have you had since beginning this workbook? How far in advance of each were there warning signs that it was coming (even if you didn't recognize the signs until later)?

3. How many slips have you had that did not become relapses? In each case, how were you able to keep it at a slip?

4. Where are slips still a significant possibility for you?

5. At this point, what are your primary motivations for overcoming addiction?

6. How do you practice coping with craving?

7. Consider the following ways to measure progress in overcoming addiction. Place two checkmarks next to those items that you think have been substantial areas of progress, one mark next to those areas of significant progress, and nothing next to those areas of little or no progress.

____level of involvement with your addiction

____level of negative consequences

____overall quality of life (level of satisfaction)

____level of self-awareness

____level of self-acceptance

____use of alternative coping methods

____ability to identify problems and make changes to solve them

____quality of relationships

____willingness to be open with trusted others

____frequency, intensity and length of cravings

____length of time between slips

____length of relapses

___level of balance in life

___ability to describe goals and values

8. Consider the following ways to determine that addiction has been overcome. Place two checkmarks next to items that you are now fully experiencing, one mark next to items that you are experiencing somewhat, and no marks next to items that you are experiencing little or not at all.

___leading your life is its own reward

___a return to addiction looks bad rather than good

___significant cravings are an experience of the past

___whatever you got through addiction you now get by less costly (and better) methods

___your life is balanced and stable

___your relationships are close and getting closer

___you are productive and even creative

___you are conceiving and moving toward even higher satisfactions

9. Review your answers to Questions 7 and 8. What conclusions do you reach?

10. If you have finished this workbook, what is the next step for you? How soon would reviewing this workbook again be useful? If you are going to review it, how will you remember to do so?

Project . . .

1. If you are ready, write out your plans for overcoming addiction. If you are ready, put these plans into effect. What do you learn from acting on these plans?

What's Important Now?

If you date your answers to these questions, the answers over time will become a diary of your growth. It is likely that in future readings of this chapter different ideas will be important to you, reflecting the fact that you are indeed changing.

Which ideas from this chapter are most useful *to you, now*?

How can you put these ideas into action?

How much confidence do you have in your judgement in selecting these ideas as crucial at this time? (Circle a number; 10 is highest confidence)

0   1   2   3   4   5   6   7   8   9   10

Notes

Notes

Appendices

Summary

Getting Started (Chapter 2)

Addiction is excessive involvement, in varying degrees, with any substance or activity. The costs of involvement clearly outweigh the benefits, but involvement continues repeatedly because it is craved. This workbook presents ideas (and techniques) for overcoming addiction which have been helpful to many others. Some ideas may be helpful to you; some may not. Ultimately, you will need to use your own judgement about which ideas to adopt. There are as many ways to overcome addiction as there are individuals. This workbook can be useful if you are ready to overcome addiction now, have overcome it but want to review your work, or are unsure about overcoming addiction and want to consider information about how to do it.

The Initial Benefits of Addiction (Chapter 3)

When you began your involvement with (what has become) your addiction, you liked the substance or activity enough to stay involved. You would not have continued unless you liked it at first. Initially the costs of involvement were probably minimal. As you continued, the costs got bigger.

The Current Benefits of Addiction (Chapter 4)

Because your initial involvement with your addiction was positive, you stayed involved long enough to develop a habit (a pattern of regular involvement with costs and benefits about equal) and eventually an addiction. Over time you came to rely on this habit or addiction as a means of coping with other problems. The addiction may now be your preferred way to cope with one or more problems. The effectiveness of your addiction as a coping method may have diminished, but you may not have realized this.

The Current Costs of Addiction (Chapter 5)

If a habit is excessively relied on as a coping method, it becomes an addiction. Although an addiction may still provide benefits, it also has costs. These costs may increase over time. Eventually they can greatly outweigh any current benefits of the involvement. Knowing and being able to recall the costs of involvement are essential to overcoming addiction.

Coping and Connecting (Chapter 6)

There are many ways to cope with any need or problem. You have identified the needs that your addiction satisfies. You could learn new coping methods, ones which would not cost as much as the addiction. There are many options for learning new coping methods. Almost all of these options involve learning from or learning with others. Learning and overcoming isolation are related projects. We need to balance learning independently with being tutored, and being independent with connecting with others.

You Have Choices (Chapter 7)

You don't *have to* overcome your addiction or change it in any way. You have choices. You have no choice about dying or certain bodily processes. You do have choice about almost everything else (even if you don't like the options available). Others may say that you "have to" change or stop your addiction, but you don't. If you are told this, the resentment you feel in response may become a problem for you. Either cutting back (moderation) or stopping altogether (abstinence) can be successful ways to overcome your addiction. Success with either will depend on your preferences circumstances, and capacity for self-control, among other factors. Your life will probably be happier if your day-to-day choices are based on your long-term goals and ultimate values.

Identifying Craving (Chapter 8)

Craving to engage in your addiction occurs at times. You experience craving because you have had repeated experience with your addiction. The craving will subside over time if your experience ends. Monitoring craving is a simple way to understand it better. Craving is partly predictable.

Understanding Craving (Chapter 9)

Cravings are time-limited. If a craving is not acted upon, it goes away. Cravings are uncomfortable, but not painful. Craving does not fundamentally interfere with your ability to make decisions. Cravings cannot force you to act on them. Craving in itself, if not acted on, is harmless. Despite the harmlessness of craving, in severe addiction we act on craving as if our survival depended on it.

Coping With Craving (Chapter 10)

Cravings are normal for you and will continue during the first weeks to months of abstinence. They may last even longer if you are moderating. You are not responsible for the existence of craving, only for your response to it. You can cope with craving by avoiding high risk situations, substituting other substances or activities, redirecting your attention, counterarguing it, or by distracting yourself. During your initial efforts at change it may be better to use avoidance and substitution. As you gain confidence, reduce avoidance and substitution, and bring out cravings regularly so that you stay in practice for dealing with them. When cravings occur spontaneously, consider them as a sign that some problem needs to be identified and solved, and as a reminder of the progress you have made. Refusing offers from others to engage in the addiction is not difficult if you are prepared.

Other Satisfactions (Chapter 11)

Before you got involved with your addiction, you experienced other satisfactions. Even during your addiction there have been other satisfactions, but you may have overlooked their significance. If you overcome your addiction, you create the opportunity to experience even better and more satisfying experiences in life. Being productive, having good relationships, and accepting yourself can be especially satisfying. If thrills are still important to you, there are other ways (less risky than your addiction) to experience them.

Building a New Life (Chapter 12)

You can build a new life that is even more satisfying than life with your addiction. The more severe your addiction, the more different your new life will be. During the initial period of overcoming addiction your primary focus will be on coping with craving. As craving diminishes ,your focus will shift to building habits which reflect your ultimate goals and values, and which enable you to experience the satisfactions that arise from these goals and values. Building good habits (positive addictions) involves observing the (good and not so good) habits of others, persistently but patiently taking small steps, revising behavior as needed to solve problems or fit larger goals, and looking beyond short-term difficulties to the long-term results you want. Your new life will also need a balance between momentary and higher satisfactions. Good health habits establish a foundation for other satisfactions.

Following Through (Chapter 13)

Regardless of whether they have been written down, you have some plans for addressing your addiction. Reviewing your plans regularly will keep them as a focus of your attention. You can notice a slip or relapse well before it actually happens. When you first notice a slip or relapse on the way, review your motivations for overcoming addiction. All relapses start as slips, but a slip does not have to become a relapse. If you follow through successfully, in time the process of following through on change, and the process of living your life, will become identical. When you arrive at this point, you will have overcome addiction!

Bibliography & Resources

Works are reviewed in the following categories:
    Books similar to this one
    Professional books
    Other books
    Catalogs
    Websites
    Software
    Faxback services

See Chapter 6 and the SMART Recovery Recommended Reading List (Appendix C) for additional reading recommendations. The support groups listed in Chapter 6 also distribute books and other media, only some of which are mentioned here. The works listed here primarily focus on substance addictions. I am not aware of comparable works on activity addictions.

-------------------- **Books Similar To This One** --------------------

Among the dozens (hundreds?) of self-help books on addiction the following three stand out as excellent choices. All focus on multiple addictions and have a scientific foundation. Comparisons between these three and my workbook are below.

Marlatt, G.A. & Daley, D.C. ***Managing Your Drug Or Alcohol Problem: Client Workbook***. San Antonio: Psychological Corporation, 1997.

This straightforward softcover workbook was intended to be used in conjunction with professional treatment. It is the shortest of the group, but it has extensive exercises (with more checklists but fewer questions than my workbook). It is intended for those who might attend 12-step or alternative groups (or no group). Brief guidance on choosing a group is given. Although encouraging its readers to resolve their substance problems entirely, it also recognizes that progress may be slow or unsteady. Although it leans toward abstinence as the preferred solution, it offers ways to measure progress that falls short of abstinence.

~~~~~~~~~~

Peele, S., & Brodsky, A., with Arnold, M. ***The Truth About Addiction And Recovery: The Life Process Program For Outgrowing Destructive Habits***. New York: Simon & Schuster, 1989.

This hardcover book has three parts. The first third is an articulate and well-referenced argument that the disease model of addiction is not only inaccurate but also damaging in many ways. The second part is a workbook on overcoming addiction (either by moderating or abstaining from substances or activities) for individuals who intend to change without professional treatment. There are many examples but fewer exercises and questions than my workbook. The workbook section alone is comparable in length to mine. The third part begins with a description of how to become more actively and constructively involved with others, and ends with a description and rationale for community action for those who feel motivated to it by the arguments presented in part one. The entire book is the longest of the four. The value of social support is a prominent theme throughout the book.

~~~~~~~~~~

Prochaska, J.O., Norcross, J.C., & DiClemente, C.C. *Changing For Good: The Revolutionary Program That Explains The Six Stages Of Change And Teaches You How To Free Yourself From Bad Habits.* New York: Morrow & Co., 1994.

This hardcover work is a popular description of the stages of change (see Chapter 2, my workbook), and the nine processes of change (embedded in my workbook in various chapters), by the psychologists who discovered and verified these concepts. The book addresses substance and activity addictions as well as psychological problems. It is aimed at self-changers, not clients in treatment, although it could also be used by them. Their approach is not disease or 12-step oriented, but the book focuses on presenting the stages and processes and their implications. One paragraph six pages before the end of the main text suggests that their approach is significantly different than the traditional one (just in case you didn't get *all* the implications!), but that appears to be the extent of direct comparison making. There are few questions or exercises but many examples.

---------------------- *Professional Books* ------------------------

Barone, D.F., Maddux, J.E., & Snyder, C.R. *Social Cognitive Psychology: History And Current Domains.* New York: Plenum, 1997.

Summarizes the research demonstrating how learning, thinking, and other cognitive processes are also thoroughly social processes.

~~~~~~~~~~

Hester, R., & Miller, W.R. (Eds.). *Handbook Of Alcoholism Treatment Approaches: Effective Alternatives.* Boston: Allyn & Bacon, 1995.

Should be in the library of every addiction treatment professional. It exhaustively reviews all randomized controlled clinical trials for alcohol problems (published as of about 1994). The remainder of the book describes the treatments that have been found to be effective. These treatments are listed in Chapter 1 of this workbook. If you want to know about what science has discovered about treatment for alcohol problems, this may be the best and most comprehensive place to start. The first chapter also reviews thirteen conceptual models for alcohol problems.

~~~~~~~~~~

Marlatt, G.A., & Gordon, J. (Eds.). *Relapse Prevention.* Guilford: New York, 1985.

An excellent summary of how a cognitive-behavioral approach to addiction (vs. a disease approach) is well-grounded in basic psychological research. It presents the acronyms AIDs and SUBTLE (see Chapter 13). This is the book I turned to (see

Chapter 6) whenever I felt discouraged about the slowness with which addiction treatment was changing.

~~~~~~~~~~

National Academy of Sciences. ***Broadening The Base Of Treatment For Alcohol Problems***. Washington, DC: Author, 1990.

The National Academy of Sciences was chartered in 1863 as the science advisor to the U.S. Congress. In the United States there is no higher authority on the application of scientific knowledge to public policy. This volume, commissioned by Congress in 1986, suggests that we need to have an extensive array of treatments for alcohol problems, not just disease model treatments, because there is no single cause of alcohol problems and therefore no single cure.

~~~~~~~~~~

National Academy of Sciences. ***Treating Drug Problems*** (Vol. 1). Washington, DC: Author, 1990.

Reviews treatments for drugs other than alcohol, and finds that they are much less well studied than alcohol treatments. It concludes that methadone maintenance is the only clearly supported treatment for drug problems, but that therapeutic communities and outpatient treatments show promise.

--------------------------- ***Other Books*** ---------------------------

Aristotle. ***Nicomachean Ethics***. (various publishers and translators; it is included in Volume 9 of *Encyclopaedia Britannica's Great Books of the Western World*). Originally written fourth century BC.

With apologies to Aristotle and scholars, this might be the original "self-help book." It considers happiness, virtue, intellectual virtues, friendship, pleasure, and related topics. It suggests that virtue is a mean between extremes (e.g., courage is a mean between foolhardiness and cowardice), and that although pleasure, honor and wealth have been proposed as the means to happiness, the contemplative life is superior. His observations remain relevant and brilliant over two millennia later, suggesting that what is fundamental about being human has changed little in that time.

~~~~~~~~~~

Fromm, E. ***The Art Of Loving***. New York: Bantam, 1963.

This classic treatise suggests that there are four solutions to the fundamental human problem of aloneness, conformity, orgiastic states, productivity and love. Productivity is possible through mindful concentration, discipline, patience and desire. In romantic love (other types are also described) the productive individual, who by definition has overcome narcissism, reaches out to care for and actively support another, based on knowledge of and respect for that individual.

~~~~~~~~~~

Kishline, A. ***Moderate Drinking: The New Option For Problem Drinkers***. New York: Three Rivers Press, 1994

The basic text of Moderation Management, including a description of how meetings run, moderation guidelines and their rationale, and a description of Ms. Kishline's experiences in abstinence-oriented treatment before she discovered the moderation option.

~~~~~~~~~

Langer, E.J. *Mindfulness.* **Reading**, Massachusetts: Addison-Wesley, 1989.

An analysis of mindlessness (making context-free judgements, having rigid categories and mindsets, prematurely making decisions), and suggestions for overcoming it. Brief descriptions about how problem drinkers who see their problem as entirely genetic tend not to take responsibility for it, and how a mindful approach to overcoming addiction would include an understanding of both advantages and disadvantages of the addiction.

~~~~~~~~~

Maisto, S.A., Galizio, M., & Connors, G.J. *Drug Use And Abuse* (3rd ed.). Fort Worth: Harcourt Press, 1998

Well-referenced and organized college textbook. Covers history of substance use, pharmacology and psychopharmacology, and treatment and prevention, for both illegal substances and caffeine, prescription and over the counter medications, alcohol and nicotine.

~~~~~~~~~

Miller, W.R., & Munoz, R.F. *How To Control Your Drinking* (rev. ed). Albuquerque: University of New Mexico Press, 1982.

Compatible with Moderation Management. Divided into three parts. First part focuses on how to handle drinking situations. Second part focuses on understanding the role drinking has in your life, and how to change that role. The last part presents 11 brief chapters on how to cope with drinkers' common problems (stress, fears, depression), etc. This book, either by itself or as part of a training, has been used in a number of published clinical trials, and has been shown to be effective in helping drinkers moderate.

~~~~~~~~~

Pinker, S. *How the Mind Works*. New York: Norton, 1997

Summarizes contemporary cognitive science, particularly as it is influenced by the theories of natural selection and the computational theory of mind. Places the presentation in Chapter 9 ("Addiction as Survival") in a broader context.

~~~~~~~~~

Plato. *Symposium* (various publishers and translators; it is included in Volume 7 of *Encyclopaedia Britannica's Great Books of the Western World*). Originally written fourth century BC.

A philosophical drama in which Socrates and his companions discuss the nature of love. Includes a description of the ladder of love (see Chapter 11, my workbook), whereby one begins with love of beautiful objects, and proceeds to love of the beauty of the mind and thought, the beauty of laws and of institutions, the beauty of science, and finally to love of beauty itself.

~~~~~~~~~~

Sanchez-Craig, M. *Drinkwise: How To Quit Drinking Or Cut Down*. Toronto: Addiction Research Foundation, 1995.

Compatible with Moderation Management. A streamlined (82 page) approach, with tear-out drinking diaries, coping diaries, and checkup forms.

~~~~~~~~~~

Siegel, R.K. *Intoxication: Life In Pursuit Of Artificial Paradise*. New York: E.P.Dutton, 1989.

Argues that the pursuit of intoxication is a fourth drive (hunger, thirst and sex being the first three). As mentioned in Chapter 5, argues that we should attempt to find a safe intoxicant. Presents the history of human involvement with common intoxicants, including their social functions, and how we learned and still learn about them by observing animal intoxication.

------------------------- *Catalogs* ----------------------------

Addiction Research Foundation
Marketing Services
33 Russell Street
Toronto, Ontario
Canada M5S 2S1
800-661-1111
416-595-6059
mktg@arf.org

ARF is a non-profit funded by the province of Ontario. Their marketing department sells both professional and public education publications. Many are more oriented to harm reduction (rather than abstinence) as compared to U.S. government publications.

The National Clearinghouse for Alcohol and Drug Information
800-729-6686 (800-SAY-NO-TO)
TDD: 800-487-4889
www.health.org

Distributes federal government publications. Most are free of charge. Has a very large selection of both professional and public education publications, and audio and video cassettes. Information specialists (some Spanish speaking) are available by phone from 8AM to 7PM Eastern time, and can help guide your selection.

------------------------ *Websites* ---------------------------

Because of the high interconnectivity of the web, only a few starting points will be listed here. See also the addresses already given in Chapter 6 or elsewhere in this Bibliography.

www.cmhc.com
        Contains a vast list of mental health and addiction resources and links.
www.cts.com/crash/habtsmrt
        HabitSmart; includes extensive information on harm reduction.
www.lobo.net/~rhester/moderat.htm
        Provides a list of North American professionals who provide alcohol moderation
        training.
www.nida.nih.gov
        National Institute on Drug Abuse.
www.niaaa.nih.gov
        National Institute on Alcohol Abuse and Alcoholism.
www.peele.net
        Author Stanton Peele's website.
www.well.com/user/selfhelp
        The Self-Help and Psychology Magazine.

--------------------------- *Software* ---------------------------

Behavioral Self-Control Program for Windows
Reid K. Hester, Ph.D.
Director, Research Division
Behavior Therapy Associates
3810 Osuna Rd NE Suite 1
Albuquerque, NM 87109
505-345-6100
505-342-2454 fax
www.lobo.net/~rhester/software.htm

Compatible with Moderation Management. Software for alcohol moderation training. Effectiveness of the software has been established by a published clinical trial.

------------------------ *Faxback Services* ------------------------

National Institute on Drug Abuse
Science-based facts on drug abuse and addiction
888-644-6432 (888-NIH-NIDA)
TTY: 888-889-6432 (888-TTY-NIDA)

Receive fact sheets by fax or mail, or listen to recorded messages (Spanish also). Covers health effects of specific drugs, drug abuse and AIDS, prevention and treatment, nationwide trends, and news releases.

SMART Recovery Recommended Reading List

See Chapter 6 for additional information about SMART. SMART also publishes a quarterly newsletter. Moderation Management does not have a recommended reading list, but books compatible with its program are noted in the Bibliography and Resources Appendix.

----------- **SMART Recovery Recommended Reading List** -----------

Core Reading List

SMART Recovery Member's Manual - A compilation of practical information designed to assist the reader in attaining the ultimate goal of recovery (1996) **

SMART Recovery: A Sensible Primer - William Knaus, Ph.D. (William Knaus, Longmeadow, MA - 3rd Revision, 1998) **

Alcohol: How to Give it Up and Be Glad You Did, A Sensible Approach - Philip Tate, Ph.D. (Rational Self-Help Press, Altamonte Spring, FL - 2nd edition, 1997) *

Addiction, Change & Choice: The New View of Alcoholism - Vincent Fox, M.Ed., CRREd. (See Sharp Press, Tucson, AZ - 1993)

When AA Doesn't Work for You: Rational Steps to Quitting Alcohol - Albert Ellis, Ph.D. & Emmett Velten, Ph.D. (Barricade Books, Inc., Fort Lee, NJ - 1992)

Changing for Good - James Prochaska, Ph.D., John Norcross, Ph.D. & Carlo DiClemente, Ph.D. (William Morrow, New York, NY - 1994)

The Truth About Addiction and Recovery - Stanton Peele, Ph.D. & Archie Brodsky with Mary Arnold (Simon & Schuster - 1989)

The Small Book - Jack Trimpey, LCSW (Delacorte Press, New York, NY - 1992)

Additional Useful Reading

How to Stubbornly Refuse to Make Yourself Miserable About Anything, Yes Anything! - Albert Ellis, Ph.D. (Lyle Stuart, Inc., Secaucus, NJ - 1988)

A New Guide to Rational Living - Albert Ellis, Ph.D. & Robert Harper, Ph.D. (Wilshire Book Company, N. Hollywood, CA - 1975)

Diseasing of America: Addiction Treatment Out of Control - Stanton Peele, Ph.D. (Lexington Books - 1989)

Heavy Drinking: The Myth About Alcoholism as a Disease - Herbert Fingarette, Ph.D. (University of California Press - 1988)

Feeling Good - David Burns (William Morrow & Company, New York, NY - 1980)

The Authoritative Guide to Self-Help Books - Santrock, Minnett, and Campbell (Guilford Press - 1994)

** Available only from SMART
* Also available from SMART

SMART Recovery Central Office,
24000 Mercantile Road, Suite #11,
Beachwood, OH 44122
phone: 216-292-0220
fax: 216-831-3776
e-mail: SRMail1@aol.com
www.smartrecovery.org

Reprinted by permission of SMART Recovery

Practical Recovery Services

"Helping You Choose Wisely"

Your community might not offer the alternative addiction services that you, having an interest in this workbook, might want. In addition to the outpatient services that I and my staff at Practical Recovery Services (PRS) offer, we are also available for long distance telephone or videophone counseling. The number of sessions needed varies. In some cases even a single consultation can be sufficient to help you move forward on overcoming addiction. Fees are based on the number and length of sessions. Credit card or other payment arrangements are available.

For individuals not living in the San Diego area we also offer the Visitor's Program (with optional Executive Package). It is an individually planned intensive outpatient experience. We arrange accommodations, some within walking distance of our offices. Inpatient detoxification or outpatient medical care is available if needed. Your treatment can include individual (or couples) sessions only, or also include participation in our addiction groups. We can keep you as busy and as intensively involved (or monitored) as you desire. On the other hand, San Diego is an excellent vacation destination, and you may desire to balance your time to include other activities.

Share Your Experiences!

It is not possible in this workbook to list the many ways to overcome addiction, and especially the multitude of coping with craving techniques. A future handbook, published as a companion to this workbook, may contain additional lists of techniques and ideas. I am continually learning new techniques from my clients. As they creatively apply in their unique situations the principles described in this workbook, they discover interesting and useful coping variations

Please send your suggestions, ideas and stories to me at the address below. Please indicate whether you would like your contribution to be acknowledged, or want it to remain anonymous. Thank you!

A. Thomas Horvath, Ph.D., FAClinP, President
(California psychologist license # PSY7732)
Practical Recovery Services
8950 Villa La Jolla Drive, Suite 1130
La Jolla, CA 92037-1705

*619-453-4777 (453-4PRS)
*619-453-5222 (tape recorded information about drop-in groups)
*619-455-0141 (FAX)
AREA CODE changes to 858 on June 12, 1999

info@practicalrecovery.com
www.practicalrecovery.com

About The Author

A. Thomas Horvath, Ph.D., FAClinP, was born and raised in Youngstown, Ohio. He graduated from St. John's College, Annapolis, Maryland, and the California School of Professional Psychology at San Diego. He is a board certified clinical psychologist (American Board of Professional Psychology) in private practice in La Jolla (San Diego), California. In 1985 he founded Practical Recovery Services, which offers an alternative to 12-step and disease oriented programs. He is a Past President of the San Diego Psychological Association and the San Diego Phobia Foundation. Since 1995 he has been President of SMART Recovery, a network of support groups for individuals abstaining from any type of addictive behavior. From 1999-2000 he will serve as President of the American Psychological Association's Division on Addictions (Division 50). The division has over 1200 members and is the world's largest organization of addictive behavior psychologists.

Index

MORE BOOKS WITH *IMPACT*

We think you will find these Impact Publishers titles of interest:

THE STRESS OWNER'S MANUAL
Meaning, Balance and Health in Your Life
Ed Boenisch, Ph.D., and Michele Haney, Ph.D.
Softcover: $13.95   208pp.
Practical verbal and graphic guide to stress management offers self-assessment charts covering people, money, work, leisure stress areas. Life-changing strategies to enhance relaxation and serenity. Emphasizes attitudes, behaviors, relaxation, eating habits, physical fitness, time management. Special emphasis on *meaning,* keeping life events in perspective, and keeping your *balance.*

THE 60-SECOND SHRINK
101 Strategies for Staying Sane in a Crazy World
Arnold A. Lazarus, Ph.D., and Clifford N. Lazarus, Ph.D.
Softcover: $12.95   176pp.
Over 100 mental health "morsels," each can be read in about a minute — provides common-sense solutions to a wide variety of problems. Introduced with a brief vignette, every item includes a discussion of the psychological implications and offers suggestions for better mental health. Learn the vital elements of a successful marriage, how to deal more effectively with anger, depression, stress, and anxiety.

IS THAT ALL THERE IS?
Balancing Expectation and Disappointment in Your Life
David Brandt, Ph.D.
Softcover: $15.95   224pp.
These are "the best of times," right? Media images promise beauty, happiness, wealth. But, many people are depressed and unhappy in their personal lives. "No era is without its disappointments," says the author, "but today we suffer from an unparalleled case of inflated hopes and expectations." The book explains the psychology of disappointment, the social influences that contribute to it, and how we can convert it to a force for positive growth.

HOW YOU FEEL IS UP TO YOU
The Power of Emotional Choice
Gary D. McKay, Ph.D., and Don Dinkmeyer, Ph.D.
Softcover: $13.95   288pp.
Puts "the power of emotional choice" within virtually everyone's reach. Straightforward procedures, practical information, and useful tools to help you take reponsibility for your emotions, enhance your awareness of feelings, and learn how to manage anger, anxiety, depression, guilt, and more. Discover how to change your ways of thinking to increase joy.

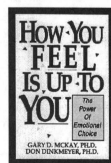

Impact Publishers®
POST OFFICE BOX 910
SAN LUIS OBISPO, CALIFORNIA 93406-0910

Please see the following page for more books.

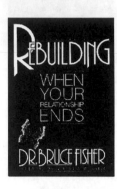